Gospel Light's

SONFORCE KIDS
SPECIAL AGENTS

On a Mission for God
DECODING JOSHUA 1:9

Teacher's Guide
Includes Reproducible Pages
Prekindergarten/Kindergarten · Ages 3 to 6

Gospel Light Vacation Bible School

Senior Managing Editor, Sheryl Haystead
Senior Editor, Heather Kempton • **Associate Editor,** Becky Garcia
Contributing Editors, Deborah Barber, Cindy Ethier, Kim Fiano, Janis Halverson, Ruthanne Swenson
Art Directors, Lori Hamilton, Samantha Hsu, Lenndy McCullough

Founder, Dr. Henrietta Mears • **Publisher,** William T. Greig
Senior Consulting Publisher, Dr. Elmer L. Towns
Senior Consulting Editor, Wesley Haystead, M.S.Ed.
Senior Editor, Biblical and Theological Issues, Bayard Taylor, M.Div.

Scripture quotations are taken from the *Holy Bible, New International Version®*.
Copyright © 1973, 1978, 1984 by International Bible Society.
Used by permission of Zondervan Publishing House. All rights reserved.

© 2007 Gospel Light, Ventura, CA 93006. All rights reserved. Printed in the U.S.A.

Contents

Teaching Helps

Sessions

Reproducible Pages

Course Description

SonForce Kids Special Agents

Invite your students to join SonForce Kids—God's courageous team of disciples standing side-by-side to serve Him. As SonForce special agents, they will follow in the words of Joshua 1:9: *Be strong and courageous. Do not be terrified; do not be discouraged, for the Lord your God will be with you wherever you go.*

The SonForce Kids headquarters is located on a satellite orbiting high above the earth. In this hi-tech command center, SonForce agents gather to prepare for their five Daily Missions: Trust! Unite! Train! Follow! Lead! Throughout VBS, your students will have the opportunity to grow in their understanding of what it means to serve God with courage as they advance from Level 1 to Level 5 agents.

From the courage shown by baby Moses' family, Level 1 agents will learn to **TRUST in God's Plans**. Following Esther's example, Level 2 agents will be encouraged to **UNITE with God's People**. To help them make wise choices like Daniel did, Level 3 agents will learn to **TRAIN for God's Service**. Just as Jeremiah obeyed God even when it was difficult, Level 4 agents will learn to **FOLLOW in God's Path**. Finally, like Joshua and Caleb, Level 5 agents will get ready to **LEAD Others to God's Promises**.

So get ready for an out-of-this-world adventure. SonForce Kids—courageous kids on a mission for God!

Basic Supplies and Equipment

Name Tags
Prepare name tags following instructions in Session 1. Place tags on a table or bulletin board near entrance so that each child can find his or her tag upon arrival and replace it at end of session.

Gadget Dog Puppet
The puppet Gadget is a dog that helps the SonForce Kids with their missions. He visits your classroom every day to participate with children in a variety of activities. (A plush dog puppet is available from Gospel Light.) To make a paper-bag dog puppet, see instructions in *Reproducible Resources*. (Optional: For added fun, hang several gadgets [small flashlight, a toy cell phone or binoculars, etc.] on Gadget's collar.)

Craft Supplies
Specific projects from *Special Agent Crafts for Kids* craft book are listed in each lesson. The craft book provides a complete list of materials and instructions for the lesson-related crafts to help children grasp each day's Bible truths in a fun-to-learn way.

Blocks
Use purchased blocks from school equipment suppliers or toy stores. Also provide toy people and animals.

CD
The songs suggested in each session are on the *SonForce Kids CD*.

Daily Schedule

SonForce Kids VBS offers five exciting sessions based on Old Testament stories that reinforce God's love and care for us. Each day presents an opportunity for children to hear Bible stories about people who loved and obeyed God. The exciting Bible stories, *SonForce Agency Manual*, lively songs, creative activities and interaction with the puppet combine to present basic concepts about God's love for children at their level.

Before Class

Teacher's Devotional
Prayerfully read each session's devotional to prepare your mind and heart for this important ministry with children. Take time to pray specifically for children and staff who have special needs.

Class Time

Adjust the length of each time segment to best fit the needs of your VBS.

Bible Learning Activity Centers • (40-45 minutes)
Welcome Time At the door, leader welcomes and assists each child in choosing an activity center.

Activities Each teacher leads activity and conversation related to the Lesson Focus in one or more activity centers. Children are free to move from one center to another. Older children may rotate from activity to activity in groups. (Note: If all children arrive at once, briefly welcome children and give a short explanation of each activity before children move to activities of their choice.) Don't worry if children don't want to participate in the suggested activity and instead create their own playtime activity (build race cars with blocks instead of building palaces, etc.). Teachers will still find the suggested conversation for each activity a helpful guide in talking about the day's focus.

Cleanup Time Teachers lead children in putting away materials.

Together Time • (10-15 minutes)
Teachers and children gather in one group for music, prayer, finger fun, a puppet activity and Bible Words.

Bible Story/Application • (15-20 minutes)
Children go to Bible story groups (about six children per teacher) or remain with entire class as one teacher presents Bible story using Bible story visuals from *Prekindergarten/Kindergarten Teaching Resources*. Then teacher and helpers sit at tables with children and guide them in completing Bible story and application activity pages from either the prekindergarten or kindergarten *SonForce Agency Manuals*.

Recreation Game/Snack • (20-35 minutes)
Teachers guide children in outdoor play activities and washup before snack. Check registration cards for any food allergies children may have. Also post a note each day alerting parents to the snack you will serve. Teachers sit with children during snack and help as needed.

Skit • (10-15 minutes)
Each day for elementary children a humorous skit is usually presented during the Opening Assembly or at another time. If prekindergarten and kindergarten children aren't included in the Opening Assembly, have skit characters visit your classroom to talk with children, or simply show the appropriate skit from *The Asteroid Incident Skit DVD*.

Craft • (15-20 minutes)
Children return to class groups or go to craft center to complete a project from *Special Agent Crafts for Kids* craft book.

Music Fun/Good-Byes • (10-15 minutes)
Children gather for music, puppet time and indoor game activities until parents arrive. Children may place stickers on the inside covers of *SonForce Agency Manuals* for saying the Bible verse of the day. Use SonForce Assortment stickers available from Gospel Light.

Decorating and Setting Up Your Room

Each day children will visit one to four Bible Learning Activity centers. With a few decorations, each center can become a special place to visit at SonForce Kids. If you do not wish to set up all the centers, use or adapt any of the following ideas to decorate your classroom. *Reproducible Resources* contains all the patterns and instructions you'll need for decorating. Remember when decorating for this age group, keep decorations at eye level so that children can enjoy seeing them.

Create a gathering place in your room for activities such as Together Time and the Bible story. Enlarge the Control Center Backdrop Pattern onto butcher paper, paint and attach to wall in front of seating area. (Optional: Place an area rug or carpet squares on floor to further designate your seating area.)

Decorating Tip

Ask people who cannot otherwise help at VBS to assist in designing and decorating your room the weekend before VBS begins.

Decorating Your Learning Centers

Use Memory Verse Posters found in *Prekindergarten/Kindergarten Teaching Resources* to decorate classroom walls or designate various classroom learning centers. The item of technology shown on each poster can be used to direct children to the center. Depending on where each poster is placed, add a few extra items to each center:

Cell Phone Poster: Place discarded cell phones in the center.

CD Poster: Add a few discarded CDs and cases. You may also attach a few to the wall or hang them from the ceiling.

Computer Poster: Set out some computer monitors, keyboards and mice. These need not be working. If a working computer is available, set the monitor to display a space-themed or star-field screensaver.

Camera Poster: Add some cameras without film or digital cameras to the center.

Sunglasses Poster: Place several pairs of sunglasses in the center for children to try on.

Entry Portal

Transform a refrigerator box into a fun entryway to your classroom. Use clear packing tape to seal all edges of closed box. Draw large, irregular-shaped archways on two opposite sides of box (see sketch). Use a utility knife to cut out archways so that kids and adults can walk through the box.

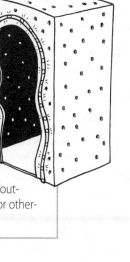

Cover inside top and sides of box with black butcher paper, or paint them black. Use scissors to punch holes in top and sides of box to create a star-field look. Line one or both archways with rope lights or Christmas lights. Place Entry Portal inside entrance to room and plug in lights. Display Welcome Poster found in *Prekindergarten/Kindergarten Teaching Resources* outside of room entrance, inside Entry Portal itself, or otherwise visible as children enter the room.

Age-Level Characteristics

SonForce Kids prekindergarten and kindergarten materials have been planned for children who are three to six years old with a ratio of one teacher for every four to six children (and can be easily adapted to include two-year-olds with a ratio of one teacher for every four children). Each activity provides enough flexibility so that young children can work successfully. Effectively instructing children of varying ages requires a teacher to recognize and accept wide individual differences in skills, abilities and interests. Regardless of the level at which a child works, a teacher can use the child's interest in the activity to guide his or her thinking toward understanding a Bible truth.

Bible Learning Activities

THREE- and FOUR-YEAR-OLDS need free play and careful supervision. They often pursue different activities, having little interest in cooperative play. Provide books and puzzles for children who are not interested in the activities offered, but engage children in conversation related to the day's lesson as they work. KINDERGARTNERS enjoy experimenting with a variety of materials and tools. Their verbal skills and enjoyment of other children make play more purposeful and interactive.

THREES and FOURS use blocks in an exploratory manner, stacking and moving them in a seemingly random fashion. Occasionally extend children's play by offering specific building instructions as suggested in the lesson. KINDERGARTNERS usually plan what they will build and then use the construction to play out an imaginary event. They incorporate accessories such as toy cars and animals in the building.

THREES and FOURS are just beginning to use art supplies and often find the finished product of little interest. Encourage them to try new things, but don't expect beauty or design. KINDERGARTNERS enjoy exploring the use of art materials but may find the process tedious after a short while. To sustain their interest, offer encouragement and assistance as needed.

Large-Group Times

THREES and FOURS need a variety of brief activities during a large-group experience. Puppets provide visual interest, but keep puppet dialogue to a minimum. Because children do not have a backlog of experiences to help them recall an idea or object, show pictures and objects to illustrate conversation and activities.

KINDERGARTNERS enjoy talking about things they have seen and done and will enjoy interacting with puppets. When the conversation relates to a common experience, most children are interested in hearing other children recount events. Avoid letting any one child dominate the conversation.

Because repetition is essential to a child's learning process, he or she needs to hear and sing the same songs again and again. Repeat familiar songs for THREES and FOURS. Introduce more of the songs suggested in each lesson for KINDERGARTNERS.

Bible Story/Application

To accommodate the attention span of THREES and FOURS, keep the Bible story very brief. Illustrate story action with visuals from *Prekindergarten/Kindergarten Teaching Resources*. Ask simple questions to help children recall Bible facts that are obvious in the story and visuals.

Although KINDERGARTNERS have a slightly longer attention span, tell the Bible stories without elaboration. They enjoy the challenge of what-do-you-think questions. (See "Storytelling Tips" on p. 9.)

Recreation Game/Snack

THREES and FOURS usually play alone or with one or two other children. They enjoy running and throwing. Competitive games are inappropriate for this age level. Each day select and use favorite games from any lesson. KINDERGARTNERS enjoy participating in games with several children. The simple games suggested in each lesson are special favorites of this age level. Because children at this age learn by repetition, we suggest that you play each game several times.

All young children enjoy preparing and eating snacks. Keep food preparation simple, with plenty of adult supervision to ensure safety. Information about children who have food allergies should be noted, and helpers who will be supervising those children should be alerted to provide alternate snacks.

Salvation of Young Children

When we have presented Jesus by both our actions and our words, a foundation is laid for a child to receive Christ as Savior. Every session may create an opportunity to talk with a young child who wants to know more about Jesus.

Jesus and Children

The young child is easily attracted to Jesus. Jesus is a warm, sympathetic person who obviously likes children, and children readily like Him. These early perceptions prepare the foundation for the child to receive Christ as Savior and to desire to follow His example in godly living. While some children at this age level (especially from Christian homes) may indeed pray to become a member of God's family, accepting Jesus as their Savior, expect wide variation in children's readiness for this important step. Allow the Holy Spirit room to work within His own timetable.

Talk Individually with Children

Something as important as a child's personal relationship with Jesus Christ can be handled more effectively alone than in a group. Ask questions that will help you determine what the child understands. Open-ended what-do-you-think questions give you a chance to hear what's really going on in the child's mind and heart. "What do you like best about Jesus?" will help a child give words to his or her thoughts and feelings about Him.

Talk Simply

Phrases such as "born again" or "Jesus in my heart" are symbolic and far beyond a young child's understanding. Focus on how God makes people a part of His family:

◇ God loves us, but we have done wrong things (sinned).
◇ God says sin must be punished.
◇ God sent Jesus to take the punishment for the wrong things we have done.
◇ We can tell God that we have done wrong and tell Him we are sorry for our sin.
◇ We can ask Jesus to be our Savior. Then we become a part of God's family.

Share this information whenever a child seems interested, but only for as long as the interest lasts. Lay a good foundation for a lifetime of solid spiritual growth!

Storytelling Tips

Before You Tell the Bible Story

1. Begin your preparation by reading the story from a current Bible translation. Although you may have read the story many times, read it again from God's Word.

2. Then read the story from this *Teacher's Guide*. This version has been prepared in words a child can understand.

3. Prepare the Bible story visuals from *Prekindergarten/Kindergarten Teaching Resources*. These visuals have been planned to reinforce and give meaning to your words. You may choose to use additional visuals such as puppets, clothespin people or a simple Bible-times costume.

4. Practice telling the story using the visual resources. If you feel it is necessary to use notes, write them on a small card and place it in your Bible. Know the story well enough so that you can look directly at the children most of the time, with only an occasional glance at your notes.

5. Keep your story brief and focused on the Bible aims. Too much information will confuse many children and extend the story length beyond their attention spans. *A good rule of thumb for telling stories to young children is to aim for one minute of story for each year of a child's age.*

When You Tell the Story

1. Place your Bible in front of you or nearby, so children recognize it as the source of the story.

2. Before you begin, be sure children are seated comfortably and can see the visuals you are using. Remove distractions such as toys or papers. Then say, "When you first came this morning, it was your turn to talk. Now it's my turn to talk and your turn to listen." Briefly remind children of activities they have done today that helped prepare them for this story. Then immediately begin with the opening sentence of your story.

3. Tell the story In your normal voice.

   ◇ Speak with confidence and enjoyment; let your genuine interest in the story come through.

   ◇ Speak distinctly and slowly.

   ◇ Change the tone of your voice to identify characters in the story.

   ◇ Create excitement by speaking slightly faster when appropriate.

   ◇ Whisper or pause briefly to create suspense.

   ◇ Use repetition and action words to maintain children's interest.

4. Enhance your story with physical expressions. Look angry or frightened. Yawn. Smile a big smile. Use the actions suggested in each story.

5. When the story ends, say your closing sentence and then stop! Conclude the story before the children lose interest. (Note: For older children, consider using the New Testament Option to connect the life of Jesus to each session's learning aims.)

After You've Concluded the Bible Story

1. Use the conversation ideas in the lesson to help review and reinforce the Bible story concepts.

2. Evaluate your storytelling experience by asking yourself the following questions:

   ◇ Did the story hold the children's attention?

   ◇ Did I know the story well enough to have eye contact with the children?

   ◇ Did I stop when the story ended?

   ◇ Did I use my visual resources so that they did not distract from the story?

3. Keep the results of your evaluation in mind as you prepare your next Bible story.

Moses: Boy in a Basket

Scripture

Bible Story: Exodus 1—2:10
New Testament Option: Luke 2—24

Lesson Focus

We can trust in God's love for us.

Bible Memory Verse

Trust in the Lord. (See Jeremiah 17:7.)

Bible Aims

During this session, each child may

1. TELL that God showed His love for Moses and his family;

2. NAME a place where he or she can remember God's love and trust in Him;

3. THANK God for His love.

Teacher Devotional

Every parent knows how stressful it can be to adjust to a new baby, but the experience of Moses' family far exceeds anything most of us will ever know. The family had a beautiful new baby boy, but Pharaoh had ordered that all Hebrew baby boys be thrown into the Nile River. Imagine trying to quiet a tiny crying baby quickly enough so that soldiers wouldn't come to kill him! As Moses grew, his parents' choices were few; if he were discovered, he would die. They did have an idea, however: They put him in the Nile in a waterproof basket. They did all they could, TRUSTING God to do something miraculous.

God had big plans for Moses. He protected Moses and used him mightily. Now think about your own life. You've seen God protect you, perhaps even through some times as dangerous as those Moses faced. Pause to consider what His plans may be for you! Those plans may not look big to you—they may even be hidden from your sight right now—but rest assured, they are of eternal importance!

There are no little plans in God's eyes. What you are doing at this moment is part of the amazing tapestry He is weaving for you and through you. In His plan, your words and actions will affect many others. He has led you and protected you just as He protected Moses. Trust in God as you watch His plans unfold!

Bible Learning Activities (40-45 minutes)

These activities are set in several centers that can be created in your classroom: Blocks, Dramatic Play, Art and the Service Project Center. (See pp. 6-7 for decorating and setup suggestions.) Select the activities for which you have the equipment, space and personnel—at least one teacher for each activity center. The activity marked ➜ will be shared during Together Time.

During Bible Learning Activity time, children may move freely around the room, participating in several activities for as long as time and interest allow.

Welcome Time

Preparation
Photocopy Name Tag Patterns onto card stock and cut out, making several of each pattern. (Optional: If choosing the pattern with black background, provide gel or glitter pens to decorate name tags.) Cut out. Punch a hole at the top of each name tag and fasten pin to tag. (Optional: Purchase theme-related name tags from Gospel Light.)

Procedure
Greet and invite each child to choose a name tag. Use permanent marker or gel and glitter pens to print child's name on tag. Assist interested children in writing their own names. Children decorate tags with crayons or markers and place stickers on name tags. (Optional: Provide SonForce Assortment stickers.) Pin tags to children's clothing. Briefly explain the activities at each center and help each child become involved in an activity.

Materials Checklist
◇ Name Tag Patterns (p. 51)
◇ colorful card stock
◇ scissors
◇ hole punch
◇ black permanent marker
◇ crayons or markers
◇ stickers

For each child—
◇ large safety pin

Optional—
◇ name tags (available from Gospel Light)
◇ SonForce Assortment stickers (available from Gospel Light)
◇ gel or glitter pens

➜ Dramatic Play Center

Caring for Baby

Preparation
(Optional: Fill bathtubs half full of water.)

Procedure
Children act out caring for babies. They pretend to wash, dress and feed them.

Conversation
God gives us many good things to eat. We can trust God to take care of us because He loves us.

>> **What does your baby like to eat, Tucker? Carrots are yummy! What is your favorite food to eat?**

>> **In our story today, we will hear about a time God showed His love for a mother who was afraid. God helped her know what to do to keep her baby safe.**

>> **Let's thank God for loving us and ask for His help to always trust Him.** Lead children in a short prayer.

Materials Checklist
◇ baby dolls
◇ items used to care for babies (baby clothes; blankets; baby dishes; empty baby-food containers; baby-sized bathtubs; empty baby shampoo containers; towels; etc.)

Block Center

River Scenes

Preparation
Cut apart Bible Block Cards. Tape each card onto a separate block. These Bible blocks will be used in upcoming VBS sessions. Cut butcher paper into river shape or use blue sheet to represent river.

Procedure
Children use blocks to outline the edges of a river and build roads coming to river. Children play with Bible blocks 1-6 to show baby Moses in the river and Miriam and the Princess taking care of Moses. (Optional: Children use toy people in real baskets to represent Moses.)

Conversation
In our story today we are going to hear about a baby inside a basket. The basket floated on a river. The baby's sister, Miriam, took care of the baby. A princess found the baby and took care of him, too. God loved baby Moses.

» **Olivia, what do you think a big sister would do to take care of a baby? God loved baby Moses.**

» **Who are the people in our class today? God loves each of us.**

Kindergarten Adaptation
Children use scissors to fringe green construction-paper rectangles to represent reeds and place along edge of river.

Materials Checklist
◇ Bible Block Cards 1-6 from *Teaching Resources*
◇ scissors
◇ tape
◇ blocks in a variety of shapes and sizes
◇ blue fabric or butcher paper

Optional—
◇ toy people
◇ small baskets

Service Project Center

Promise Cards

Preparation
To make Promise Cardholders, prefold and then unfold one sheet of white paper for each child as shown in sketch.

Fold top corners in.

Fold bottom half of page up to top.

Procedure
Show and describe your sample Promise Card and Cardholder. Give each child two index cards and prepared Cardholder. Children decorate their Promise Cards and Cardholders using markers, stickers and paper scraps. Write promises dictated by each child on his or her cards. (I will hug my mom. I will call my grandma. I will feed my dog.) Children refold their Cardholders and help tape side closed. Children place Promise Cards inside pockets of Cardholders.

Conversation
We're so glad God loves us! We can show God's love by helping others. Today we are making Promise Cards that we can give to people in our family. Our Promise Cards tell something we will do to help at home.

» **Caden, who will you give your cards to?**

» **Savannah, thank you for helping Lilly pick up the markers. Helping your friends is a way to show God's love. What is another way you can help in our classroom?**

Kindergarten Adaptation
Help interested children print promises on their own.

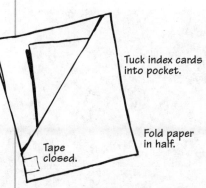

Tuck index cards into pocket.

Fold paper in half.

Tape closed.

Materials Checklist
◇ 8½x11 (21.5x28 cm) white paper
◇ markers
◇ stickers
◇ construction-paper scraps
◇ tape

For each child—
◇ 2 white, unlined index cards
◇ glue

Art Center

Play-Dough Kids

Preparation

Mix flour, salt, water, food coloring and dishwashing liquid in large bowl. Knead mixture until soft and pliable. If dough is sticky add more flour. If dough is too stiff, slowly add more water. (Recipe makes enough dough for six children.) Cut construction paper into 6-inch (15-cm) squares, making two or three for each child.

Procedure

Children roll balls of dough to form people shapes. They decorate paper squares to represent places they go (their house, school, church, grocery store, the park, etc.). Children move shapes between places.

Conversation

Let's use our dough to make play-dough kids. Then we'll put our play-dough kids in different places they might go.

>> **Alex, tell me about the place you drew. What do you like to do at the park? God loves you when you are at the park and God loves you when you are at home. That means that wherever you go, you can remember that God loves you.**

>> **Our Bible says,** *Trust in the Lord.* **That means you can know that God will always love you. Let's pray and thank God for loving us.** Invite volunteers to pray, "Thank You, God, for loving me."

Kindergarten Adaptation

Instead of drawing places on paper squares, children use construction paper, scissors, markers, tape, etc. to make places. They dictate names of places for you to write on each paper square.

Materials Checklist

◇ 3 c. flour
◇ 1 c. salt
◇ 1¼ c. water
◇ food coloring
◇ 3-4 squirts dishwashing liquid
◇ large bowl
◇ scissors
◇ construction paper in various colors
◇ ruler
◇ markers

CLEANUP TIME

Signal Cleanup Time by playing a song from *SonForce Kids CD*. Involve children in cleanup by bending to their eye level, calling each child by name, and giving one simple direction at a time.

Together Time (10-15 minutes)

For younger children, use only the activities marked ♦.

♦ Song
Play "Be Strong and Courageous" from *SonForce Kids CD*. Sing song once with children. Then sing again and lead children in motions while singing song.

♦ Welcome/Gadget Puppet
Puppet enters. **Hello boys and girls. My name is Gadget. Who has a dog at home? What kinds of games do you play with your dog?** Volunteers respond. **I play with the SonForce Kids and help them every day. We play lots of games together.**

I want to learn everyone's names today, so we are going to play a game that will help me learn what your names are. Let's say this rhyme together.

> **Welcome to our class today! I am so glad you came.**
> **When the beanbag comes to you, stand up and say your name.**

Children repeat the rhyme and pass the beanbag around the circle until all children have said their names. **I'm so happy that you are here at SonForce Kids VBS this week and that we can play games together. Bye.** Puppet exits.

Show Moses Poster. **At SonForce Kids VBS we're going to learn that God loves us and we can always trust Him. Let's learn a finger play that tells about God's love.**

♦ Finger Play: "God's Love"

God gives me food to eat each day,

And many places where I can play.

A home where I can grow and live,

And people who have love to give.

God gives me stars that shine above.

Thank You, God, for Your great love!

Younger Child Adaptation: Omit the third and fourth lines to shorten the finger play.

Sharing
Some of you pretended to take care of babies today. Pretend to rock a baby if you have a baby brother or sister. What are some things you have to do to take care of a baby, Cameron? Babies can't take care of themselves. They trust us to feed them and keep them warm. We can trust God to take care of us when we need His help, too. We can always trust God because He loves us.

♦ Bible Verse
Hold Bible open. **Listen to what our Bible tells us.** *Trust in the Lord.* Children repeat verse. **When you trust the Lord, it means you know that God will always love you. We can always remember and trust in God's love!**

Song
Play "With Love" from CD. Lead children in singing and doing motions found in songbook DVD.

♦ Prayer
Let's talk to God. Closing your eyes will help you think about God while you talk to Him. Let's thank God for His love. Pray and thank God for loving each child.

♦ Transition
Today we are going to hear a story about how God showed His love for Moses and his family.

◇ Bible
◇ *SonForce Kids Songbook, CD* and player
◇ Gadget Puppet (available from Gospel Light, or make puppet as described in *Reproducible Resources*)
◇ Moses Poster from *Teaching Resources*
◇ beanbag
Optional—
◇ items to hang on Gadget's collar (small flashlight, toy cell phone, toy binoculars, etc.)

Bible Story/Application (10-15 minutes)

(Note: See "Storytelling Tips" on p. 10 for ways to present the story.)

(Note: See "Storytelling Tips" on p. 10 for ways to present the story.)

Preparation

Before class, prefold *SFA Manual* pages to form storybooks, and then reopen pages. In class, children will find it easier to refold the page.

Moses: Boy in a Basket

(Hold Bible open to Exodus 1 as you expressively tell the story. Do motions and show flannel figures as indicated.)

Hold up Bible. **What is this book called?** Children respond. **The stories in the Bible are all true.** Show basket. **What are some things you could put in this basket? Listen to hear a story from the Bible that tells what a mother put into her basket.**

A New Baby

A long time ago, a girl named Miriam was very happy to get a new baby brother! Each day Miriam and her family took good care of the baby. (*Show Figure 1.*) They played with him. They rocked him. (*Pretend to rock baby.*) They patted him when he went to sleep. The baby's family loved him!

But not everyone was happy that this baby had been born. The king of that land wanted to be mean. He sent his soldiers to find the babies and take them away. (*Make sad face.*) But this baby's family loved and trusted God, and God gave THIS baby's mother an idea! (*Make happy face.*)

The Baby Is Hidden

"I'll make a basket just the right size for my baby," Mother said. "I'll fill in every little hole in the basket, so water can't get in. Then the basket will float. I'll put some warm blankets inside it." Mother got the basket all ready. (*Show Figure 2.*) Then she laid her baby in the basket, very gently. (*Pretend to lay baby in basket.*) She and Miriam carried the basket to the river and put it into the water.

"Miriam, watch our baby in the basket," Mother said. So Miriam stayed near the basket. She hid in the bushes by the river. She watched and waited. (*Show Figure 3.*)

The Baby Is Found

While Miriam was watching, she heard some women walking down to the river. Miriam peeked through the grass to see who they were. (*Pretend to pull grass apart and look through.*) It was the PRINCESS—the king's daughter—and her servants! They were coming to the river to take a bath. Would they see the basket? What would they do with the baby inside?

"What's that basket doing in the water?" one servant asked.

"Bring it to me," the princess said. (*Show Figure 4.*)

Miriam must have held her breath! She watched as the princess opened the basket. Then the baby cried. (*Make crying sound.*) The princess felt sorry for him.

Quickly Miriam came from her hiding place. She ran to the princess. "Would you like me to find someone to take care of this baby for you?" she asked. (*Show Figures 5 and 6.*)

"Yes!" answered the princess. "This baby will need someone to take care of him." So Miriam ran. And who do you think she brought back to the princess? Her own mother! (*Lead children to clap hands.*)

The princess named the baby Moses. She made sure the king's soldiers didn't hurt him. The princess even PAID Moses' mother to take care of her own baby! The baby was safe and the family was VERY glad to have their baby back home again. (*Make happy face.*) They were happy that God loved and cared for their baby boy.

Conclusion

God showed His love for Moses and his family. God kept Moses safe. God loves us, too. We can always remember and trust in God's love. Lead children in prayer saying, **Dear God, thank You for loving us and always taking care of us. Help us to always trust You, no matter where we are. In Jesus' name, amen.**

New Testament Option

God showed His love for us by sending Jesus to Earth. Choose one of the storytelling options found on the back of the Life of Jesus Poster to tell children how God sent Jesus to show His love for us.

Materials Checklist

◇ Bible
◇ Life of Jesus Poster from *Teaching Resources*
◇ Figures 1-6 from *Teaching Resources*
◇ *SFA Manual* Level 1 pages
◇ flannel board
◇ basket
◇ crayons or markers (including green, blue and yellow)

Application

Teachers and helpers sit at tables with children. Pass out *SFA Manual* pages and crayons or markers. Children fold pages to make mini-storybooks.

To review the Bible story, children follow along in their mini-storybooks as you read the story aloud. **What did Moses' family do to take care of Moses?** (Made a basket. Watched over him.) **Who came to the river to find the baby?** (The princess.) **God showed that He loved Moses! God kept Moses safe. I'm glad that we can remember God loves us and cares for us.**

Children unfold mini-storybook and repeat Bible verse with you. **God loves us wherever we go.** Children complete "God Loves Me" activity. **Where is a place you go? What are some times kids might feel afraid? God loves us and helps us, even when we're afraid.**

Recreation Game (10-15 minutes)

Jumpin' the River

Preparation

Lay ropes on floor approximately 1 foot (0.3 m) apart to represent a river. Stuff paper bags with newspaper and tie closed with yarn to create rocks. Place rocks in river.

Procedure

In our Bible story today, Moses' mother and sister kept him safe by hiding him in a basket on a river. Let's see if we can cross this river. Children stand several feet from river and take turns to run and jump over it, avoiding touching any rocks. After all children have taken a turn, move one rope to make a slightly larger river. Children jump over river again. Keep moving the rope until it becomes too difficult for children to jump over the river. Then move the ropes closer together in stages and children jump again until river is its original size.

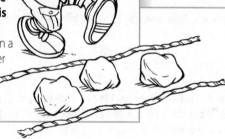

Materials Checklist

◇ 2 jump ropes
◇ ruler
◇ paper bags in various sizes
◇ newspaper
◇ yarn

Snack (10-20 minutes)

Moses in a Basket

Preparation

Mix several drops blue food coloring into cream cheese or frosting. Melt $\frac{1}{2}$ cup butter in saucepan. Add 1 cup brown sugar and boil, stirring for 3 to 5 minutes. Add 5 ounces of chow mein noodles. Divide mixture into 12 muffin cups and then use a metal spoon to press an indentation into each cup to form a basket shape.

Procedure

Children wash and dry hands. **Who has seen a river? Today we are going to make rivers and baskets that we can eat.** They frost top of graham cracker with blue cream cheese or frosting, swirling it to look like a river. Then they remove baskets from muffin cups and place on top of graham-cracker rivers.

Children place a jellybean inside their baskets to represent baby Moses.

Note: Check registration forms for possible food allergies and post a note alerting parents to the food items used in today's snack.

Materials Checklist

Food items—
◇ cream cheese or frosting
◇ blue food coloring
◇ butter
◇ brown sugar
◇ chow mein noodles
◇ graham crackers
◇ jelly beans

Utensils—
◇ saucepan
◇ large spoon
◇ foil muffin cups
◇ metal spoon
◇ paper plates
◇ plastic knives
◇ napkins
Serves 12.

Craft (15-20 minutes)

Baby Moses in a Basket

Children make Baby Moses in a Basket craft. For complete craft instructions, see *Special Agent Crafts for Kids*.

Music Fun/Good-Byes (10-15 minutes)

After children complete their crafts, guide them to the music activity area. Play CD as children gather.

Song

Play "Be Strong and Courageous" from *SonForce Kids CD*. Lead children in singing song and doing motions found in songbook DVD.

Game

Place five or six baby items on tray. **What could you use the items on this tray for? Moses' mother probably didn't have these things to take care of Moses. But, I'm going to show you some things moms and dads use today to take care of babies.** After children have looked at items on tray for several seconds, hide tray and remove one item. Show tray again and then ask, **What is missing from the tray? That's right, Alicia, the baby bib is missing. Very good!** Continue game as time and interest allow. For variation, hide items around classroom. At your signal, children find hidden items and place on tray. When all items have been found, children close their eyes while you hide items again.

Bible Verse

Today we've learned that God loves us. We can always trust in God's love wherever we are. Open Bible. **Our Bible says, *Trust in the Lord*. Let's say our Bible verse together and clap when we say each word.** Lead children to repeat verse.

Prayer

Let's pray to God and thank Him for loving us. Children repeat phrases of prayer after you. **Dear God, thank You for Your love. Thank You for loving us no matter where we are. In Jesus' name, amen.**

Good-Bye/Gadget Puppet

Puppet enters. **What did you like best today at SonForce Kids? There is still so much to do and to see that you will have to come back tomorrow! We'll play more games together. Bye-bye!** Remove children's name tags and distribute take-home materials. (Optional: Play songs from *SonForce Kids CD* and provide rhythm instruments for children to play until parents arrive.)

Esther: Queen at Risk

Scripture

Bible Story: Esther 2—8
New Testament Option: Luke 2—24

Lesson Focus

We can help others.

Bible Memory Verse

With love, help each other. Galatians 5:13

Bible Aims

During this session, each child may

1. **TELL** how Esther and her friends helped each other;

2. **NAME** a way that he or she can help others;

3. **ASK** for God's help to look for times he or she can help others.

Teacher Devotional

During the rule of Xerxes (also known by the Hebrew name Ahasuerus) of Persia occurs the beautiful and charming story of Esther. Although God's name is not mentioned in the book of Esther, His presence can be found behind each word. God has a part in all the events of human life.

Esther stands out as God's chosen one. The beauty of Esther was that she wasn't spoiled by her great position. Though she became queen of a great king, she didn't forget the kindness of her cousin Mordecai, who had brought her up from childhood. Esther was faced with the opportunity to help rescue the lives of her oppressed people, the Jews, but only at great risk to her own life. Accepting this dangerous task, she carried it out with courage and wisdom. Even as she went forward on behalf of the Jews, she asked them to pray and fast on HER behalf. Esther knew that God was listening to the prayers of His people and that with His help they could UNITE and defeat their enemy.

It was a daring act for her to enter unsummoned into the presence of the king. Yet she knew she must choose the right course, despite the danger to herself. She knew this was a time to have courage and stand up for others. Esther was prepared and was brought to the kingdom for just such an hour.

We would all do well to pause and ask, "Why has God allowed me to live at this particular hour?" When faced with challenges that require the courage to do what is right, it is always easier when we are supported by the prayers of fellow believers.

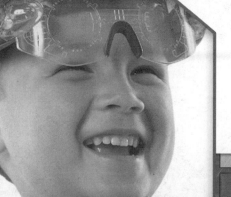

2 **UNITE** With God's People

Bible Learning Activities (40-45 minutes)

The activity marked ➜ will be shared during Together Time.

Welcome Time

Personally greet each child and assist him or her in putting on a name tag. Guide children in choosing which Bible Learning Activity to participate in first.

Service Project Center

VIP Crowns
Preparation
Photocopy onto card stock two sets of Crown and Extender Patterns for each child and cut out. (Note: Premade crowns can be purchased from craft or party-supply stores.) Cut streamers and rickrack into small pieces. Place rickrack, streamers, jewels and foam stickers into shallow containers.

Procedure
Children make two crowns, one to keep and one to give away. They glue decorations onto crowns and, with teacher's help, staple extenders to back of the crowns as shown in sketch.

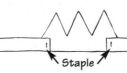

← Staple →

Conversation
Today you can make one crown to wear and one to give to someone you love.

>> **Who are some people that wear crowns?** (Kings. Queens.) **When we wear crowns we feel special, like a king or queen.**

>> **Jayce, who will you give your crown to? Your grandpa is a very special person. God loves your grandpa and God loves you. Our Bible says,** *With love, help each other.* **What is a way that you help your grandpa? Helping your grandpa clean the kitchen is a way to show God's love. What is a way that you can help someone here at SonForce Kids VBS?**

Kindergarten Adaptation
With teacher's help, children use markers to write, "You are special" or "You are a VIP" on crowns.

Materials Checklist
◇ Crown Pattern (p. 52)
◇ Extender Patterns (p. 52)
◇ card stock in various colors
◇ scissors
◇ streamers
◇ rickrack in metallic colors
◇ fake jewels
◇ markers, gel pens, glitter pens
◇ peel-and-stick geometric foam stickers (available from craft and school-supply stores)
◇ glue sticks
◇ stapler

SERVICE PROJECT OPTION
Children make crowns to give to a senior center or an organization in the community that cares for families in need.

→ Block Center

Esther's Palace

Procedure

Children build Bible-times palaces. They use fabric pieces to decorate walls and floors of palace. Children use cylinder-shaped blocks to make pillars and rectangle-shaped blocks to build walls around palaces. They use toy people and Bible blocks to move people in and around palaces and show Esther talking to the king.

Conversation

A house for a king and queen is called a palace. In our story today we are going to hear about a brave queen named Esther. Esther loved God. Esther asked the king to help her and her friends.

>> Let's help each other build houses that kings and queens live in. Ava, you chose a pretty silver fabric to put in your palace.

>> Corinne, thank you for helping Bryan put away the big blocks. What is another way you and Bryan can help someone here at SonForce Kids VBS? Lead child in a short prayer asking God to help him or her look for ways to help others.

Dramatic Play Center

Let's Have a Party!

Preparation

Cut streamers into 12-inch (30.5-cm) lengths.

Procedure

Play music from *SonForce Kids CD*. Children decorate for a party. They tape streamers around play area. Children serve toy food, put on dress-up clothes, hats, shoes and jewelry to pretend to have a party. (Optional: Children serve cheese slices and crackers.) Children use toy cameras to take pictures of each other.

Conversation

In our story today we are going to hear about a brave queen named Esther who helped God's people. Esther celebrated with a big party. Let's pretend we are having a party.

>> When is a time you had a party at your home?

>> What are some things you did to help get ready for the party? (Decorate. Set the table. Get dressed up.)

Kindergarten Adaptation

Provide small gift boxes, gift wrap, tape and child-sized scissors. Children wrap pretend gifts to take to the party.

Art Center

Helping Mural

Preparation

Tape a piece of black or blue butcher paper to table. Put collage materials on paper plates.

Procedure

Children help each other glue collage materials onto butcher paper in designs of their choosing. Talk with children about ways they can help each other. (Note: When finished, display the mural in classroom. At the end of the day or when VBS ends, cut out a section so that each child can take a section home.)

Conversation

Today we are going to work together and help each other make a pretty picture.

>> **What will you glue onto our picture, Tyler?**

>> **Ryan, thank you for helping Annie reach the markers. Our Bible says,** *With love, help each other.*

>> **Cole, you saw that Mikayla knocked over the glue. Thank you for picking it up. You are doing what God says when you help your friends.**

Kindergarten Adaptation

On their section of the mural, children use neon or gel pens to write the names of people they can help.

Materials Checklist

◇ black or dark blue butcher paper
◇ tape
◇ collage materials (metallic chenille wire, large sequins, paper in various colors and textures, gel and glitter markers, colored chalk, tissue paper, fabric scraps, wallpaper scraps, etc.)
◇ paper plates
◇ glue sticks
◇ scissors

CLEANUP TIME

Signal Cleanup Time by playing a song from *SonForce Kids CD*. Involve children in cleanup by bending to their eye level, calling each child by name and giving one simple direction at a time.

Together Time (10-15 minutes)

For younger children, use only the activities marked ♦.

♦ Song

Play "Listen to Advice" from *SonForce Kids CD*. Sing song once with children. Then sing again, leading children in motions found in songbook DVD.

♦ Welcome/Gadget Puppet

Puppet enters and greets children. **I'm ready to play another game! Let's play one of my favorites, *Doggie, Doggie, Where's Your Bone*? You can help each other find my bone. When the "Doggie" looks for my bone, you can bark once if Doggie guesses wrong and twice if Doggie guesses right.** Choose one child to be "Doggie." Children sit in a circle. Doggie covers his or her eyes and children pass dog biscuit. At your signal, children stop passing biscuit. Child with biscuit holds it behind his or her back. Doggie opens his or her eyes and tries to guess which child is holding biscuit. Continue play until all children have had a turn. (Note: For large groups of children, use three or four dog biscuits.) To finish game, child holding bone gives it to Gadget Puppet. **Thanks for helping me find my bone. I think I'll go eat it now! Bye-bye.** Puppet exits.

Today at SonForce Kids VBS we are learning that we can help others. You don't have to be a grown-up to help others. Let's say a rhyme that will remind us of ways that WE can help.

♦ Finger Play: "Two Hands"

I have two hands. They help all day!

Two hands to put my toys away.

Ten fingers here for helping (Mother),

Ten fingers here for helping others.

Five fingers here, five fingers there

To fold like this for quiet prayer.

♦ Prayer

God loves us, and wants us to show His love by helping others. Pray aloud with children, **Dear God, thank You for loving us. Help us look for times when we can help others. In Jesus' name, amen.**

Sharing

Alexis, you helped Vanessa build a big palace. God is glad when we help our friends. We can help our friends, even when it is hard. When is a time it might be hard to help a friend? (When I'm playing a game. When I'm watching TV.) **We can ask God to help us look for ways we can help our friends.**

♦ Bible Verse

Hold Bible open. **Listen to what our Bible tells us:** *With love, help each other.* Children repeat the verse. **God loves us and helps us. He wants us to help others. What are some ways you can help your family?** (Set the dinner table for my mom. Help feed and take care of my cat, Bailey.) **I'm glad we can help our families.**

Song

Play "With Love" from CD. Lead children in singing and doing motions found in songbook DVD.

♦ Transition

In our Bible story today, you are going to hear about how a brave queen and her friends helped each other.

Materials Checklist

◇ Bible
◇ *SonForce Kids Songbook, CD* and player
◇ Gadget Puppet
◇ real or card stock dog biscuit

Bible Story/Application (10-15 minutes)

(Note: See "Storytelling Tips" on p. 10 for ways to present the story.)

(Note: See "Storytelling Tips" on p. 10 for ways to present the story.)

Materials Checklist

◇ Bible
◇ Life of Jesus Poster from *Teaching Resources*
◇ Figures 7-12 from *Teaching Resources*
◇ *SFA Manual* Level 2 pages
◇ flannel board
◇ paper or toy crown
◇ crayons or markers

Preparation

Before class, prefold *SFA Manual* pages to form storybooks, and then reopen pages. In class, children will find it easier to refold the page.

Esther: Queen at Risk

(Hold Bible open to Esther 2 as you expressively tell the story. Do motions and show flannel figures as indicated.)

Show crown. **Who wears a crown? Kings and queens usually wear crowns. Listen to find out what a special queen in Bible times did.** (Note: For added interest, place crown on your head while you tell story.)

A New Queen

When Esther was a child, her father and mother died. (*Show Figure 7.*) So Esther went to live with her cousin Mordecai (MOR-dih-ki). He took care of Esther. (*Show Figure 8.*) Esther and Mordecai were Jews who lived far away from their own country. God's people were called Jews.

Esther grew to be a young woman. One day, the most amazing thing happened! King Xerxes (ZUHRK-sees) chose Esther to be his new queen! (*Clap hands. Show Figures 9 and 10.*) After that, Esther lived in the palace. The king must have given her a lot of beautiful clothes and jewelry.

The king had a helper named Haman. (*Show Figure 11.*) The king was so pleased with Haman that he made a law that said EVERYONE had to bow down to Haman. Bowing down to someone was a way to show how important that person was.

Esther's cousin, Mordecai, knew that God was more important than any person. He loved God. (*Show Figure 8.*) So Mordecai wouldn't bow down to Haman. Haman was so angry with Mordecai that he wanted to kill him. (*Make angry face.*) And because Mordecai was a Jew, Haman wanted to kill ALL Jews! Haman tricked the king into making a law to kill all the Jews. (*Lead children to say "Boo!"*)

A Scared Queen

When Esther heard about the law, she didn't know what to do. (*Show Figure 9.*) Haman and King Xerxes did not know that she was a Jew. She wanted to talk to the king about Haman's plans, but she was afraid. (*Make scared face.*) Anyone who tried to talk to the king without being invited could be killed—even the queen! The King had not invited Esther to come and see him for many days.

Esther may have thought, *Haman doesn't know I'm a Jew. Maybe I will be safe.* (*Show Figure 8.*) But Mordecai warned her, "Even though you are the queen, you will not escape. You must talk to King Xerxes. Maybe this is why God made you queen."

A Brave Queen

Esther said, "Even though I am afraid, I will go to the king. But first, I will ask God for help. For three days, I won't eat anything. I will spend my time praying to God instead." Esther asked all of the Jews in the city to help her by praying, too. For three days, Esther, Mordecai and all the other Jews prayed and did not eat anything. Then Esther got dressed up with her beautiful clothes and jewelry. (*Pretend to put on jewelry.*) When she walked through the door where the king was, she wondered what he would do. (*Show Figure 10.*) But when the king saw her, he SMILED and held out his royal scepter to welcome her.

Esther asked the king and Haman to come to a dinner with her. Haman was happy to hear he was going to have dinner with the queen! So King Xerxes and Haman came to Esther's dinner. (*Rub stomach. Show Figure 12.*) Esther told the king that someone was going to KILL all of her people. Esther cried, "Please save my life and the lives of all my people." The king got ANGRY. (*Make angry face.*) He asked, "Who would DO such a thing?"

Esther pointed at Haman. "The man who wants to do this is HAMAN!" King Xerxes had Haman taken away! The king asked Esther to write a new law to keep the Jews safe. All God's people were VERY happy! They had a big party to celebrate! (*Clap hands and lead children to shout "Yippee!"*)

Conclusion

God helped Esther to be brave and go see the king, even though she was afraid. Esther helped God's people. God will show us ways we can help others, too. Lead children in prayer, saying, **Dear God, thank You for loving us. Help us to look for ways to help others. In Jesus' name, amen.**

New Testament Option

Jesus showed His love by helping others. Choose one of the storytelling options found on the back of the Life of Jesus Poster to tell children that Jesus helped others.

Application

Teachers and helpers sit at tables with children. Pass out *SFA Manual* pages and crayons or markers. Children fold pages to make mini-storybooks.

To review the Bible story, children follow along in their mini-storybooks as you read the story aloud. **What did Haman plan to do because he hated Mordecai?** (Kill Mordecai and all of the Jews.) **How did Esther help God's people?** (She told the king about Haman. She helped make a new law so that God's people would not be hurt.) **How did God's people help Esther?** (They prayed for her.) **Esther was brave to go to see the king. Esther asked for God's help and He helped her. God loves us and He will always help us, too.**

Children unfold mini-storybook and repeat Bible verse with you. **God loves us and wants us to show His love by helping others. He will give us courage to help, even when it might be hard.** Children complete "My Helping Puzzle" activity. **What is a way you can help your friend who is sick? How about your mom or dad? We can ask God to help us look for ways to help others.** Allow volunteers to name other people they can help.

Recreation Game (10-15 minutes)

Royal Races

Preparation

Use masking tape, chalk or rope to mark a starting line. Cut three simple crown shapes from construction paper or use the Crown Pattern on page 52 of this book.

Procedure

In our Bible story, a brave queen helped her people. Queens and kings wear crowns. Today, we are going to wear crowns while we race. Divide class into two teams. Choose one child to be the king. King stands at opposite end of play area, wearing a crown and holding a scepter. Give the first child on each team a crown. At your signal, child puts crown on his or her head, runs to touch king's scepter and then runs back to team. Child hands crown to next in line. He or she runs to king and touches scepter, and then runs back to team and hands crown to next child in line. Game continues in relay fashion until each child has had a turn.

Materials Checklist

◇ masking tape, chalk or rope
◇ 2 royal scepters (rulers, glitter sticks, etc.)
◇ 3 sheets of construction paper
◇ scissors
◇ stapler

Snack (10-20 minutes)

Queen Esther's Crown

Preparation

Make rice crispy bars, following package directions. Cut into 16 rectangles, about 4x3 inches (10x7.5 cm) in size. Cut crown shapes from rectangles (sketch a). Pour candies into separate bowls.

Procedure

Children wash and dry hands. They use icing tubes to decorate their crowns and then press candies onto icing (sketch b).

Note: Check registration forms for possible food allergies and post a note alerting parents to the food items used in today's snack.

Materials Checklist

Food items—
◇ 13.5-oz. box of crispy rice cereal
◇ 5½ c. minimarshmallows
◇ ¼ c. butter or margarine
◇ cooking spray
◇ small candies such as gumdrops, M&Ms, candy sprinkles, silver candy balls, licorice laces, etc.
◇ icing tubes

Utensils—
◇ 12x17-inch (30.5x43-cm) jelly roll pan or cookie sheet
◇ knife
◇ paper plates
◇ paper bowls
◇ plastic knives
◇ napkins
Serves 16.

Craft (15-20 minutes)

Jeweled Wristband

Children make Jeweled Wristband craft. For complete craft instructions, see *Special Agent Crafts for Kids*.

Music Fun/Good-Byes (10-15 minutes)

After children complete their crafts, guide them to the music activity area. Play CD as children gather.

Song

Play "Be Strong and Courageous" from *SonForce Kids CD*. Lead children in singing song and doing motions found in songbook DVD.

Game

Children sit together in a circle. Give each child a block. Put one block on the floor in the middle of the circle. **Today we are going to use our blocks to help build a tall tower.** Children then take turns stacking their blocks on top of the block in the center, working together to build a tower without causing the blocks to fall. If tower falls, children start again. Continue game as time and interest allow. (For added fun, give one or two children an oddly shaped block.)

Bible Verse

Open your Bible. **Our Bible says, *With love, help each other*. Let's say the verse softly.** Children repeat verse quietly. **Now, let's say it a little louder.** Continue repeating verse a few times until children are saying verse with loud voices. If time permits, repeat verse a few times, getting quieter each time until children are whispering.

Prayer

Today we talked about ways to help others. Let's ask God to help us find ways to help each other, even when it might be hard. Jack, who is someone you can help at home? Grace, what is a way you could help someone here at SonForce Kids VBS? Pray and ask God to help children look for ways to help the people they named.

Good-Bye/Gadget Puppet

Puppet enters. **Wow! What a busy day! We learned a lot about helping each other today. Hold up one finger. Tonight when we go home, let's try to help someone in one special way! I can't wait to see you all tomorrow! Bye.** Remove children's name tags and distribute take-home materials. (Optional: Play songs from *SonForce Kids CD* and provide rhythm instruments for children to play until parents arrive.)

Daniel: Servant of God

Scripture

Bible Story: Daniel 1
New Testament Option: Luke 2—24

Lesson Focus

We can do what is right.

Bible Memory Verse

Listen to advice and you will be wise. (See Proverbs 19:20.)

Bible Aims

During this session, each child may

1. **TELL** that Daniel loved God and did what was right;
2. **IDENTIFY** ways that he or she can do what is right;
3. **ASK** God's help to do what is right.

SonForce Kids
Special Agents
LEVEL 3
TRAIN

Teacher Devotional

Imagine living through an enemy attack that destroys your home and makes you a prisoner of war. Daniel and his friends lived through just this horror, probably while they were still teenagers. The best and brightest of Jerusalem's royal court, they saw their promising futures and privileged circumstances evaporate as they left Jerusalem behind.

Captive in a strange land, they were without a country or a chosen future. The Babylonians were clearly working to eliminate their Israelite identities and make them ready to serve Nebuchadnezzar. The boys probably had no choice about being dressed in Babylonian fashion or given Babylonian names. But there was one way they could hold on to who they really were: They could honor the dietary laws of Israel. It may seem like a small thing to us, but it was one way to be obedient and remain true to the training they had received to serve God.

God often brings such small acts to our attention, acts we can do to continue to put into practice our love and obedience to God. These small acts may not seem any more significant than the food choices of Daniel and his friends. It's usually easier to ignore such small things and go along with "the program." But remembering the ways in which we have been trained will help us obey God with the courage of Daniel. When we're tempted to go along with the crowd, God gives us courage and strength to stand up for His ways like Daniel and his friends did.

Bible Learning Activities (40-45 minutes)

The activity marked ➜ will be shared during Together Time.

Welcome Time

Personally greet each child and assist him or her in putting on a name tag. Guide children in choosing which Bible Learning Activity to participate in first.

Service Project Center

Place Mats

Preparation

Photocopy and cut out two or more copies of Place Setting Patterns for each child. Cut four or five food pictures from magazines for each child.

Procedure

Children glue food pictures onto Plate Patterns. Children glue Plate Patterns onto 18x12-inch (45.5x30.5-cm) construction-paper rectangles to make place mats. They use markers to color Spoon, Fork, Knife and Napkin Patterns and glue onto mats (see sketch). (Optional: Use Con-Tact paper to laminate place mats.) Children make extra place mats as time and interest allow.

Conversation

Today you may each make place mats to take home and give to people you love.

➤➤ **Sophia, who will you give one of your place mats to? What is your favorite food? God loves us and He gives us many good things to eat.**

➤➤ **Landon, thank you for giving Paige some markers and not keeping them all yourself. You did what is right. Doing what is right is a way to show God's love to others. What is another way you will do what is right during cleanup time?**

Younger Child Adaptation

Children draw and color food items on Plate Patterns rather than gluing pictures from magazines.

Kindergarten Adaptation

Children cut out their own plates, utensils and napkins.

Materials Checklist

◇ Place Setting Patterns (pp. 53-54)
◇ scissors
◇ food magazines
◇ construction paper in various colors
◇ markers
◇ glue sticks

Optional—
◇ clear Con-Tact paper

SERVICE PROJECT OPTION

Children make place mats to give to a senior center or an organization in the community that cares for families in need.

Block Center

Table Builders

Procedure
Children build tables using blocks. They set tables with toy dishes or paper plates and place Bible blocks 15-18 and toy vegetables on plates. Children use toy people and Bible blocks 12-14 to pretend to eat vegetables. If time permits, children may also use blocks to build palaces.

Conversation
In today's Bible story, Daniel and his friends did what was right by following God's rules. They ate the food God told them to eat.

>> Samuel, what is your favorite vegetable? I like peas, too.

>> Our Bible says, *Listen to advice and you will be wise.* When we listen to our parents and obey them, we are listening to good advice. The Bible tells us that listening to advice will make us wise. Being wise means you do what God says is good and right.

Kindergarten Adaptation
Children cut pictures of vegetables from food magazines and place pictures on block tables.

Materials Checklist
◇ Bible Block Cards 12-18 from *Teaching Resources*
◇ blocks in various shapes and sizes
◇ toy dishes or small paper plates
◇ plastic or toy vegetables
◇ plastic or toy people

→ Dramatic Play Center

Vegetable Gardens

Preparation
Tape empty seed packets closed. Use tape to make several 2x3-foot (.6x.9-m) rectangles on the floor. (Note: Remove tape immediately when finished with activity.)

Procedure
Children pretend to plant gardens in masking-tape rectangles. Children care for gardens using seed packets, gardening equipment and clothing and toy vegetables.

Conversation
In our Bible story today we will hear about how a man named Daniel did what was right by following God's rules.

>> Hailey, thank you for sharing the rake with Morgan. When you share with others you are doing what is right. What are some other things you can share?

>> What vegetables are you growing in your garden, Ewan? You are taking good care of your corn and squash. God loves us. He gives us many yummy foods to eat!

>> Let's ask God to help us to always obey Him and do what is right. Lead children in a short prayer.

Kindergarten Adaptation
Children put vegetable stickers on index cards to create labels for vegetables they are putting in their gardens. Provide markers for interested children to copy the names of vegetables from seed packets onto labels.

Materials Checklist
◇ empty vegetable seed packets
◇ masking tape
◇ measuring stick
◇ child-sized gardening equipment (spades, rakes, watering cans, etc.)
◇ child-sized gardening clothing (hats, gloves, overalls, boots, etc.)
◇ plastic or toy vegetables

Art Center

Juice Painting

Preparation

Buy juices. (Optional: Press juice from fresh vegetables using a juicer.) Pour juices into shallow containers and dilute using a small amount of water.

Procedure

Children put on smocks or shirts. Children press firmly with white crayons to draw pictures (happy faces, stick figures, etc.) or designs on finger-paint paper. They use paintbrushes dipped in juice of their choosing and paint over paper to reveal pictures.

Conversation

In our Bible story today, we are going to hear about four friends who did what was right by obeying God's rules.

>> **Delaney, you are using the orange-colored juice to paint your picture. What vegetable did your juice come from? Carrots are good to eat, too.**

>> **Thank you for waiting for a paintbrush, Zach. When you wait for a turn you are doing what is right. You show your love for God when you do what is right. What are some other things you can do to show you love God?** (Tell the truth. Be kind. Help someone who is hurt.)

Younger Child Adaptation

Children paint pictures of their choosing with vegetable juice instead of using crayons to draw pictures first.

Materials Checklist

◇ several kinds of vegetable juices (carrot, beet, tomato, etc.)
◇ shallow containers
◇ water
◇ paint smocks or old shirts
◇ finger-paint paper
◇ white crayons
◇ paintbrushes
Optional—
◇ juicer

CLEANUP TIME

Signal Cleanup Time by playing a song from *SonForce Kids CD*. Involve children in cleanup by bending to their eye level, calling each child by name and giving one simple direction at a time.

Together Time (10-15 minutes)

For younger children, use only the activities marked ♦.

♦ Song
Play "Listen to Advice" from *SonForce Kids CD*. Sing song once with children. Then sing again, leading children in motions found in songbook DVD.

♦ Welcome/Gadget Puppet
Puppet enters and greets children. **I'm so glad, we get to play another game together. In today's game you must ask carefully so that you do what is right.** Children play a game like Mother May I. Children line up on one side of the room. Stand on the opposite side of the room from children. First player says "Gadget, may we take two steps?" Answer, "Yes, you may." All children take two steps. Children continue asking permission, varying the number of steps from one to five, until all children have crossed the room to you. If children forget to ask permission, they all take the same amount of steps back. **Sometimes it is hard to remember to ask the right way, but you all did great! I have to go now. I think I need a nap. Bye!** Puppet exits.

Today at SonForce Kids we are learning about doing what is right. Let's say a rhyme to remind us to do what is right.

♦ Finger Play: "Do What Is Right"

Two eyes to see what is right to do,

Two lips that smile the whole day through,

Two hands that put the toys away,

A tongue that says kind words each day,

Two feet that run to help someone

Makes doing right a lot of fun!

Sharing
Some of you worked in a vegetable garden this morning. Wyatt, what vegetables did you plant? You were kind to give some carrots to Paul. When you are kind, you are doing what is right. God is glad when we do what is right.

♦ Bible Verse
Hold Bible open. **Our Bible tells us, *Listen to advice and you will be wise.*** Children repeat verse. **What does it mean to be wise?** (You do what God says is good and right.) **What is a way that you can do what is good and right, Riley?** (Obey my mom and dad. Listen to my teacher.) **Listening to your mom and dad is a way you can listen to good advice. Our Bible says that is how we can be wise.**

Song
Play "Hear the Word" from CD. Lead children in singing and doing motions found in songbook DVD.

♦ Prayer
God wants us to do what is right. Let's ask Him to help us. Pray aloud with children, **Dear God, thank You for loving us. Please help us to do what is good and right. In Jesus' name, amen.**

♦ Transition
In our Bible story today we are going to hear about four boys who obeyed God's rules about what food to eat.

Bible Story/Application (10-15 minutes)

(Note: See "Storytelling Tips" on p. 10 for ways to present the story.)

Preparation
Before class, prefold *SFA Manual* pages to form storybooks, and then reopen pages. In class, children will find it easier to refold the page.

Daniel: Servant of God
(Open Bible to Daniel 1 and place Bible in front of you. Read story from *God Helps Me Obey* big book.) Show vegetables. **What are the names of these vegetables? Listen to hear why a boy and his friends decided to eat only vegetables.**

Many years ago, a boy named Daniel lived in Jerusalem. Daniel loved God and obeyed His rules. One day, a king from a country called Babylon came with a strong army. His army took many people from Jerusalem back to Babylon. Daniel and his three friends were taken. They walked for days and days, until they finally came to Babylon.

Daniel and His Friends Are Chosen
The king told all the wisest boys, "You come and live with me.
I'll train and feed you for three years, and then we all will see—
We'll see who are the wisest and the strongest boys of all.
I'll pick the best to be my helpers; now grow strong and tall!"
Daniel and his three best friends were chosen by the king
To read and grow and eat good food and learn all kinds of things.
One day, Daniel and his friends were given the king's meat.
But this food had first been offered at an idol's feet!

Daniel and His Friends Do What Is Right
So Daniel went and told the guard, "We cannot eat this meat!
We'll obey God. We'll grow and learn with vegetables to eat!"
The guard said, "No! The king wants all you boys to eat his food!
I'll be in trouble if you don't. The king won't think it's good!"
Brave Daniel said, "For just 10 days, please put us to the test:
We'll eat the food God tells us to, then see who looks the best!"
The guard agreed, so vegetables and water were their food.
Their cheeks were pink; their eyes were bright. The boys just grew and grew!
The boys obeyed by following God's rules for 10 short days.
They looked so healthy and so strong! The guard was quite amazed!
The four friends followed all God's rules. They grew up wise and strong.
They showed the king that following God's rules is never wrong.

Daniel and His Friends Are Wise
When it was time to choose his helpers out from all the best,
The king said Daniel and his friends were 10 times better than the rest!
Like Daniel and his friends, you are important in God's eyes—
Obey God's rules and talk to Him so that you can be wise!
The king's food looked and smelled very good. But God had told His people not to eat certain foods. And the king's food was not something they could eat. Daniel and his friends loved God. They chose to do what was right and obey God's rules.

Conclusion
Daniel and his friends showed their love for God by doing what was right. We can show our love for God by doing what is right, too. Our Bible says, *Listen to advice and you will be wise.* **A person who is wise does what is right and good—things that God wants us to do. Let's ask God to help us do what is right so that we can be wise.** Lead children in prayer, saying, **Dear God, thank You for loving us. Help us to show our love for You by doing what is right. In Jesus' name, amen.**

New Testament Option
When Jesus lived on Earth, He did what was right. Choose one of the storytelling options found on the back of the Life of Jesus Poster and talk with children about how Jesus did what was right.

Materials Checklist
◇ Bible
◇ Life of Jesus Poster from *Teaching Resources*
◇ *God Helps Me Obey* big book from *Teaching Resources*
◇ 2 or 3 vegetables (corn on the cob, carrot, mushroom, etc.)
◇ *SFA Manual* Level 3 pages
◇ crayons or markers

Application

Teachers and helpers sit at tables with children. Pass out *SFA Manual* pages and crayons or markers. Children fold pages to make mini-storybooks.

To review the Bible story, children follow along in their mini-storybooks as you read the story aloud. **How did Daniel and his friends show their love for God?** (By obeying God's rules and not eating the king's meat.) **What did the king do when he saw Daniel and his friends?** (Chose them to be his special helpers.) **God loves us. We can show our love for Him by doing what is right, just like Daniel did.**

Children unfold mini-storybook and repeat Bible verse after you. **God wants us to learn to do what is right and good. God will help us do what is right.** Children complete "Do What Is Right" activity. **What are some ways you can do what is right?** (Say kind words to others. Wait patiently to play with the toy cars. Clean my room without complaining.)

Recreation Game (10-15 minutes)

Vegetable Soup

Procedure

Today's story tells about four boys who obeyed God by following His rules about what food to eat. In our game, we are going to use vegetables to pretend to make soup. Give each child a spoon and a vegetable. (Optional: Use plastic or toy vegetables instead of real ones.) Children stand at one end of playing area. Place box at other end of playing area. When you say "Go!" each child places his or her vegetable on spoon, walks quickly to pot or box, drops in vegetable and returns to you to receive another vegetable. Continue play until all vegetables have been placed in pot or box.

Kindergarten Adaptation

Divide group into two teams and play as a relay using only two spoons. Give each child a vegetable. First child in line puts vegetable on spoon and takes his or her vegetable to pot and then quickly returns and passes spoon to next child in line. Continue game in relay fashion. Team that puts all of its vegetables in the pot first wins.

Materials Checklist

◇ stock pot or large box

For each child—

◇ soup spoon or ladle
◇ several small, raw vegetables (baby carrots, celery, new potatoes, pea pods, green beans, pearl onions, radishes, etc.)

Optional—

◇ plastic or toy vegetables

Snack (10-20 minutes)

Veggie Daniel

Preparation

Cut tomatoes into round slices. Cut other vegetables into small pieces. Place each type of vegetable in a separate bowl. Fill paper cups half-full with dip.

Procedure

Children wash and dry hands. Children arrange vegetables into people shapes on paper plates, using plastic knives to cut them into smaller pieces if necessary. Children then dip vegetables into dressing and enjoy!

Note: Check registration forms for possible food allergies and post a note alerting parents to the food items used in today's snack.

Materials Checklist

Food items—

◇ tomatoes
◇ other vegetables, such as celery and carrot sticks, broccoli and cauliflower florettes, parsley, zucchini, sliced mushrooms and olives, etc.
◇ ranch dressing or any favorite vegetable dip

Utensils—

◇ cutting board
◇ knife
◇ bowls
◇ 3-oz. disposable cups
◇ paper plates
◇ plastic knives
◇ napkins

Craft (15-20 minutes)

Veggie Concentration

Children make Veggie Concentration craft. For complete craft instructions, see *Special Agent Crafts for Kids*.

Music Fun/Good-Byes (10-15 minutes)

After children complete their crafts, guide them to the music activity area. Play CD as children gather.

Materials Checklist

◇ Bible
◇ *SonForce Kids Songbook, CD* and player
◇ Gadget Puppet

Song

Play "Listen to Advice" from *SonForce Kids CD*. Lead children in singing song and doing motions found in songbook DVD.

Game

Provide pictures from grocery advertisements and magazines of both food and non-food items (toys, etc.). Volunteers take turns to select and show a picture to the group. If the item is edible, children pat their stomachs and nod their heads. If item is inedible, children shake their heads no. If the answer is no ask, "What should we do with it instead?"

Bible Verse

Open your Bible. **Our Bible says, *Listen to advice and you will be wise*. Heather and Kevin, you can say our Bible verse with me. Steve and Becky, you can say our Bible verse with me now.** Continue until all children have had a turn.

Prayer

God can help us do what is right. Let's ask Him to help us. Children repeat phrases of this prayer after you. **Thank You, God, for loving us. Help us to show Your love to others by doing what is right. In Jesus' name, amen.**

Good-Bye/Gadget Puppet

Puppet enters. **Who is coming back to SonForce Kids VBS tomorrow? I'll be here, too, ready to learn more from the SonForce Kids and have fun playing some new games. Good-bye boys and girls.** Remove children's name tags and distribute take-home materials. (Optional: Play songs from *SonForce Kids CD* and provide rhythm instruments for children to play until parents arrive.)

Jeremiah: Prophet in Trouble

Scripture

Bible Story: Jeremiah 36—39
New Testament Option: Luke 2—24

Lesson Focus

We can obey God, even when it is hard.

Bible Memory Verse

Obey me, and I will be your God. Jeremiah 7:23

Bible Aims

During this session, each child may

1. **TELL** that Jeremiah obeyed God, even when it was hard;
2. **DESCRIBE** a time when he or she can obey God;
3. **THANK** God for His love and ask for God's help to obey Him.

Teacher Devotional

Jeremiah was called from the obscurity of his native town to assume, at a critical hour in the nation's life, the overwhelming responsibilities of a prophet. His father, Hilkiah, was a priest, so Jeremiah inherited the traditions of an illustrious ancestry. His early life was likely also influenced by strong religious leaders. But God had something even better for Jeremiah than to spend his life as a priest serving at the altar. God appointed this young man to be a prophet of the Lord in this trying hour in the history of the Chosen People.

Frequently, the Israelites chose to disobey God, even though God's commands had been designed for their well-being. When they stopped following God, they ended up in great trouble. So God warned them through Jeremiah's messages. Just as the people of Israel had to choose whether or not they would listen to the warning in Jeremiah's messages, people today face the choice between following God's ways or pursuing their own ways.

The God of Jeremiah is always ready to give each one of us, and the children we teach, the courage we need to follow in His path, even in difficult circumstances. God's promise of courage springs from His love. He is ready to forgive us when we make a wrong choice, and even better, He is fully able to help us follow Him wholeheartedly so that we can live in the best way possible!

4 **FOLLOW** In God's Path

Bible Learning Activities (40-45 minutes)

The activity marked ➜ will be shared during Together Time.

Welcome Time

Personally greet each child and assist him or her in putting on a name tag. Guide children in choosing which Bible Learning Activity to participate in first.

Service Project Center

Thank-You Cards

Preparation
Cut card stock in half lengthwise and then fold widthwise to make one blank note card for each child. Place collage materials and stickers in shallow containers.

Procedure
Children glue collage materials onto front of cards and use stickers and markers to decorate. Each child chooses someone to give Thank-You Cards to and, with teacher's help, writes name of person on card and signs name.

Conversation
It is important to say thank-you when someone has helped you or done something kind. Today we are making cards to give to people who have helped us.

➤➤ **Who will you give your card to, Tim? How do your granddad and grandma help you? Your granddad and grandma love you. God loves you, too.**

➤➤ **When you use kind words to tell someone thank-you, you are obeying God, Gabriel. What is another way you can obey God here at SonForce Kids VBS? God is glad when we obey Him.**

Kindergarten Adaptation
With teacher's help, children write "Thank you for" on cards. Then write specific messages on cards for children. (Teaching at VBS. Helping me. Making my snack.)

Materials Checklist

◇ 8½ x11-inch (21.5x28-cm) card stock in various colors
◇ scissors
◇ collage materials, such as string, buttons, bits of chenille wire, tissue-paper squares, etc.
◇ various stickers
◇ shallow containers
◇ glue sticks
◇ markers

SERVICE PROJECT OPTION
Children make decorative cards to give to a senior center or an organization in the community that cares for families in need.

Art Center

Pretty Names

Preparation

Cut a length of butcher paper and tape it onto table. Use marker to write, "I can obey God" in large letters on paper. Write each child's name in block letters randomly on paper (see sketch). Cut tissue paper into 2-inch (5-cm) squares.

Procedure

Children decorate their names by gluing tissue-paper squares in block letters. Children may also use markers and glitter pens to fill in the outlines of their names. After children have decorated butcher paper, roll into scroll and tie with length of yarn. Use scroll as prop when telling Bible story. (Note: At the end of class time, cut around each child's name and give to him or her to take home.)

Conversation

Our Bible says, *Obey me, and I will be your God*. Sometimes it is hard to obey God.

>> **What color did you choose to decorate your name, Angelina? Thank you for giving Rosa the purple marker. Sharing is a way to obey God's Word.**

>> **What is a way that you can obey God?** (Share my dolls with my little sister. Listen and come when my mom calls.) **God is glad when we obey Him. Let's thank God for His love and ask Him to help us always obey Him, even when it is hard.** Lead child in a short prayer. **Dear God, thank You for loving me. Help me to always obey You. In Jesus' name, amen.**

Younger Child Adaptation

Children decorate whole page, not just names.

Materials Checklist

◇ butcher paper
◇ tape
◇ scissors
◇ markers
◇ glitter pens
◇ tissue paper in various colors
◇ glue sticks
◇ yarn

→ Dramatic Play Center

Lovely Letters

Preparation

Fold flaps closed on cardboard box and tape closed. Cut a slit in side of box to make a mailbox. Cut paper into several 4-inch (10-cm) squares for each child. Cut mailing labels into several 2-inch (5-cm) squares for each child.

Procedure

Children use markers to color pictures and "write" letters on paper squares. They color mailing labels to create stamps and put stamps on envelopes. Children fold letters, put in envelopes, seal and place in mailbox.

Conversation

Who has received a letter from someone? Today we are pretending to write and send messages to people that we love. In our Bible story we are going to hear about a man named Jeremiah who obeyed God's Word. Jeremiah delivered a message to a king who was not kind.

>> **Tell me about your letter, Katie. What did you write? Who will you send your letter to? Writing and sending messages is fun.**

>> **Jose, thank you for making a stamp for Katie's letter. You were being kind and helping your friend. When you are kind, you are obeying God's Word.**

Materials Checklist

◇ cardboard box
◇ tape
◇ scissors
◇ ruler
◇ various types of paper (construction, copier, card stock, etc.)
◇ markers
◇ envelopes in various sizes
◇ white mailing labels
◇ large paper bag with handles

Block Center

Temple Builders

Preparation

Use construction paper, toilet paper rolls and yarn to make several scrolls for the block area. Cut paper into one 4½ x 12-inch (11.5x30.5-cm) rectangle for each scroll you are making. Cut yarn into one 12-inch (30.5-cm) length for each scroll you are making. Tape one end of paper rectangle to a toilet-paper tube. Then tape the other end of paper to another tube as shown in sketch. Using yarn or ribbon, tie closed. Cut cardboard into several rectangular pieces so that children can put doors on temple.

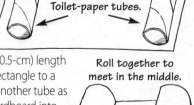
Toilet-paper tubes.

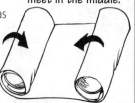
Roll together to meet in the middle.

Procedure

Children use blocks to build temple walls. They tape cardboard pieces to blocks to make doors for the temple. Children move Bible blocks in and out of temple to tell story of Jeremiah and his helper writing God's words on a scroll. They unroll and re-roll scrolls and pretend to read messages.

Conversation

In Bible times, people wrote words on scrolls instead of in books. A scroll was a long piece of paper. In today's story we are going to hear about a man named Jeremiah who obeyed God. Jeremiah told his friend to write God's words on a scroll. Then the king heard the words on the scroll.

» **Tell me about what you are building, Luis. Thank you for waiting patiently for the long blocks. Sometimes it is hard to be patient, but when you are patient you are obeying God.**

» **When is another time it might be hard to be patient? To share? Let's pray and ask God to help us obey Him, even when it is hard.** Lead children in short prayer.

Kindergarten Adaptation

Children use markers to write the word "Bible" or to write their names on scrolls.

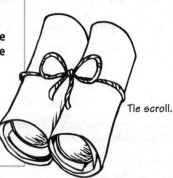
Tie scroll.

Materials Checklist

◇ Bible Block Cards 19-23 from *Teaching Resources*
◇ scissors
◇ ruler
◇ construction paper in various colors
◇ empty toilet-paper rolls
◇ tape
◇ yarn or ribbon in various colors
◇ lightweight cardboard
◇ blocks in various shapes and sizes

CLEANUP TIME

Signal Cleanup Time by playing a song from *SonForce Kids CD*. Involve children in cleanup by bending to their eye level, calling each child by name and giving one simple direction at a time.

Together Time (10-15 minutes)

For younger children, use only the activities marked ♦.

♦ Song
Play "Be Strong and Courageous" from *SonForce Kids CD*. Sing song once with children. Then sing again, leading children in motions found in songbook DVD.

♦ Welcome/Gadget Puppet
Puppet enters and greets children. **Are you ready to play another game with me? In today's game we need to listen to instructions. Let's play a game like Simon Says, but since I will tell you what to do, we'll call it Gadget Says.** Puppet leads children in game. Give children actions that are related to dogs. (Gadget says, "Bark three times." Gadget says, "Scratch like you have fleas." "Run like a dog." "Wag your tail.") **Isn't it fun to be a doggie? I have to go now. It's time for my doggie training. Bye!** Puppet exits.

   At SonForce Kids VBS today we are learning about obeying God's Word. God is glad when we obey. Let's say a rhyme that reminds us that we can obey.

♦ Finger Play: "Annie, Annie"
*Annie, Annie, what can you do,
With the hands God made for you?
I can use my hands to obey,
I can use my feet the same way.

*Seth, Seth what can you do,
With the eyes God made for you?
I can use my eyes to obey,
I can use my mouth the same way.

*Laurel, Laurel what can you do,
With the ears God made for you?
I can use my ears to obey,
I can use my arms the same way.

*Substitute with names of children in your classroom. Discuss with children ways to use different body parts to obey. (I can use my mouth to say kind words. I can use my ears to listen. I can use my eyes to see and help others.)

Sharing
Some of you wrote messages today! Ethan, I saw you help Sadie put her letter in our mailbox. When you help others, you are obeying God's Word.

♦ Bible Verse
Hold Bible open. **When are some times you can obey God at home? In the car? Listen to what our Bible tells us.** *Obey me, and I will be your God.* **God loves us and He will help us when it is hard to obey.** Children repeat verse.

Song
Play "Hear the Word" from CD. Lead children in singing and doing motions found in songbook DVD.

♦ Prayer
Let's ask God to help us always obey Him. Lead children in prayer saying, **Dear God, thank You for loving us. We love You. Help us to always obey You, even when it might be hard. In Jesus' name, amen.**

♦ Transition
Our Bible story today tells about a man who obeyed God, even when a powerful king was angry with him.

Bible Story/Application (10-15 minutes)

(Note: See "Storytelling Tips" on p. 10 for ways to present the story.)

See "Storytelling Tips" on p. 10

Preparation
Prefold *SFA Manual* pages to form storybooks, and then reopen pages. In class, children will find it easier to refold the page.

Jeremiah: Prophet in Trouble
(Open Bible to Jeremiah 36 as you expressively tell the story. Do motions and show flannel figures as indicated.)

What words or letters do you know how to write? Listen to find out about some words a man wrote down.

Jeremiah Obeys
Jeremiah was a man who loved and obeyed God. (*Show Figure 13.*) One of the ways in which Jeremiah obeyed God was by telling people messages from God. Jeremiah was called a prophet.

Jeremiah told the people God's message that they should love and obey God. But the people did not love and obey Him. (*Look sad.*)

God still loved the people. He wanted them to stop doing what was wrong. He knew that very bad things would happen if they kept doing wrong. So God told Jeremiah to write down God's very important words.

Jeremiah called for his helper, Baruch (BEHR-uhk). (*Show Figure 14.*) Jeremiah said the messages from God out loud. Baruch wrote the messages down on a scroll. A scroll is like a long rolled-up sheet of paper with writing on it. (*Show scroll made earlier in Art Center.*)

The King Does Not Obey
"Take the scroll to the Temple and read it to the people," Jeremiah told Baruch. The Temple was the place where God's people came to pray and learn about God.

Baruch took the scroll to God's Temple. He read it in a loud, clear voice. (*Show Figure 15.*) Some people went to King Jehoiakim (juh-HOY-uh-kuhm) and told him about the scroll.

The king ordered one of his helpers to bring the scroll to him. One of the king's helpers read it to him. But the king did not want to stop doing wrong things. The king did not want to start obeying God's words.

The king was angry about what God's words said! (*Look angry.*) The king grabbed a knife. He cut the scroll apart. He burned each piece in the fire! (*Pretend to cut and toss scroll. Show Figure 16.*)

The king may have thought he had gotten rid of God's words. But God told Jeremiah, "Write the scroll again." Jeremiah and Baruch obeyed God. They wrote another scroll just like the first one. (*Show Figures 13 and 14.*)

The People Do Not Obey
Baruch read the scroll to the people again. (*Show Figure 15.*) But the king and the people did not listen. (*Look sad.*) They kept doing what was wrong, so the bad things God said would happen, did happen.

Conclusion
It is sad that the king and the people did not obey God. But it's good that Jeremiah obeyed God and tried to help others learn about God's Word. We can obey God, too. Our Bible says, *Obey me, and I will be your God.* Lead children in prayer. **Let's ask God for His help to obey. Dear God, thank You for Your love. Please help us to always obey You, even when it might be hard.**

New Testament Option
When Jesus lived on Earth, He obeyed God. Choose one of the storytelling options found on the back of the Life of Jesus Poster to tell children how Jesus obeyed God.

Materials Checklist
◇ Bible
◇ Life of Jesus Poster from *Teaching Resources*
◇ Figures 13-16 from *Teaching Resources*
◇ *SFA Manual* Level 4 pages
◇ Pretty Names scroll made in Art Center
◇ crayons or markers

Application

Teachers and helpers sit at tables with children. Pass out *SFA Manual* pages and crayons or markers. Children fold pages to make mini-storybooks.

To review the Bible story, children follow along in their mini-storybooks as you read the story aloud. **What did Jeremiah do to obey God?** (He listened to God and told his helper to write down what God said.) **What did the king do when he heard God's words?** (He cut up the scroll and burned it.) **What did Jeremiah do next?** (He obeyed God and wrote the words down again.) **Jeremiah obeyed what God said to do, even when it was hard. We can obey what God tells us to do, too. We can find ways to obey God by reading and listening to God's Word, the Bible.**

Children unfold mini-storybook and repeat Bible verse after you. **When is a time that it might be hard for you to obey God at your home?** Volunteers respond. **God can help you obey Him, even when it is hard.** Children complete "Way to Obey!" activity. **What are some ways you can show God's love and obey here at SonForce Kids VBS?** (Say kind words, even when my friend has been unkind. Put away the blocks, even when I want to keep playing.)

Recreation Game (10-15 minutes)

Pass the Scroll

Preparation

Tightly roll both ends of card stock inward to make a scroll. Wrap rubber band around scroll to help keep it closed.

Procedure

In today's story, we heard about a man who obeyed God and wrote God's words on a scroll. Let's play a game using a scroll. Play a game like Hot Potato. Children sit or stand in a circle. Play music from CD. Children pass the scroll around the circle as quickly as possible while music is playing. When music stops, the child holding the scroll calls out, "I will obey God!" Be ready to help each child have a turn to get the scroll.

Younger Child Adaptation

When the music stops, all children together call out, "I will obey God."

Kindergarten Adaptation

Write "I will obey God" on the card stock sheet. When the music stops, the child holding the scroll unrolls it and reads the words aloud. (Note: Eliminate rubber band.) Child then re-rolls scroll and play continues.

Materials Checklist

◇ *SonForce Kids CD* and player
◇ sheet of card stock
◇ rubber band

Snack (10-20 minutes)

Jeremiah's Scroll

Procedure

Children wash and dry hands. They peel fruit leather from backing and place on plate. (Optional: Before peeling fruit leather from backing, children use icing tubes to write words on them.) They place one pretzel rod on each end of fruit leather and roll ends together to form a scroll (see sketch). Children tie scrolls closed using licorice laces.

Note: Check registration forms for possible food allergies and post a note alerting parents to the food items used in today's snack.

roll ends together

Materials Checklist

Food items—
◇ fruit-leather roll-ups
◇ pretzel rods
◇ licorice laces
Optional—
◇ icing tubes in various colors
Utensils—
◇ paper plates
◇ napkins

Craft (15-20 minutes)

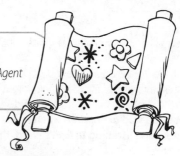

Jeremiah's Scroll

Children make Jeremiah's Scroll craft. For complete craft instructions, see *Special Agent Crafts for Kids*.

Music Fun/Good-Byes (10-15 minutes)

After children complete their crafts, guide them to the music activity area. Play CD as children gather.

Song

Play "Listen to Advice" from *SonForce Kids CD*. Lead children in singing song and doing motions found in songbook DVD.

Game

Lead children in practicing ways to say yes and no with different parts of their bodies. **One way to say yes is to nod our heads.** Nod head with children. **We can say no by shaking our heads.** Shake head with children. Repeat with other body parts (elbows, shoulders, feet, etc.). For instance, children wave elbows up and down to say yes and wave elbows back and forth to say no. Ask children simple questions. **Do you like pizza? Answer with your elbows!** Children answer by waving their elbows up and down or back and forth.

Bible Verse

Today we've learned that God is glad when we obey. Our Bible verse says, *Obey me, and I will be your God*. **Obeying means that we say yes to what God tells us to do. God loves us and will help us to obey Him.**

Prayer

Let's pray and thank God for loving us and ask Him to help us obey. Children repeat phrases of prayer after you. **Dear God, thank You for loving me. Help me to always obey You, in Jesus' name, amen.**

Good-Bye/Gadget Puppet

Puppet enters. **We had fun today. What did you like best? I can't wait to come back tomorrow and spend time playing games with you all. I have to go and do some doggie exercises now. It's important to stay in shape when you help the SonForce Kids. Bye.** Puppet exits. Remove children's name tags and distribute take-home materials. (Optional: Play songs from *SonForce Kids CD* and provide rhythm instruments for children to play until parents arrive.)

Joshua: Spy in a Strange Land

Scripture

Bible Story: Numbers 13—14:9
New Testament Option: Luke 2—24

Lesson Focus

We can have courage because God promises to always be with us.

Bible Memory Verse

Be strong and courageous ... for the Lord your God will be with you wherever you go. Joshua 1:9

Bible Aims

During this session, each child may

1. **TELL** that Joshua and Caleb believed God's promise;

2. **REPEAT** God's promise from the Bible that tells God will be with us wherever we go;

3. **THANK** God for the promises in His Word.

SonForce Kids
Special Agents
LEVEL 5
LEAD

Teacher Devotional

The book of Joshua provides a wealth of encouragement and wisdom for the followers of God. Yet this book is not only about following God but also about leading others to Him. As we follow the story of Joshua, we see a man who is determined to trust God's promises and equally determined to lead His people to receive those promises.

Picture this scene: The children of Israel have recently been freed from slavery in Egypt and are on the verge of inheriting the Promised Land. But, because of their fear, the poor Israelites are ready to turn back to the slavery they have just left behind. They cannot invade this land filled with "giants" and take the walled cities. The conquest of the land seems impossible!

Now, Caleb and Joshua had seen the same "giants" and had inspected the same fortifications, yet they insisted that the land could be taken! Because of their courage and trust in God's promises, they were ready to LEAD these people.

God sometimes calls us to lead others in fearful situations, too. When He does, we have the same words that were given to Joshua in answer to his prayer for help in his great undertaking: *Be strong and courageous. Do not be terrified; do not be discouraged, for the Lord your God will be with you wherever you go* (Joshua 1:9). These words are just as true for us!

5 **LEAD**
Others to God's Promises

Bible Learning Activities (40-45 minutes)

The activity marked ➜ will be shared during Together Time.

Welcome Time

Personally greet each child and assist him or her in putting on a name tag. Guide children in choosing which Bible Learning Activity to participate in first.

Service Project Center

Giveaway Bags

Preparation
Photocopy onto card stock one Tag Pattern for each child and cut out. Place food items and spoons in separate bowls. Cut ribbon into one 6-inch (15-cm) length for each child.

Procedure
Children wash and dry hands. They choose food items and spoon items into plastic bags. Children use heart-shaped stickers to decorate bags. With teacher's help, they punch holes in top corners of plastic bags and in Tags. Children use markers to write name of person they want to give bag to on Tag. They then sign Tags, and with teacher's help, tie Tags onto bags.

Conversation
God loves us and He wants us to show His love to others.

>> **Emmit, thank you for giving Candace the purple heart sticker. You are showing God's love when you share with your friends. Who will you give your bag to?**

>> **What are some ways you can show God's love to others here at SonForce VBS, Angelina? God is glad when we share with others. When you share your Giveaway Bag with someone, you are showing God's love.**

Kindergarten Adaptation
Provide child-sized scissors for children to cut out their own Tag Pattern.

Materials Checklist

◇ Tag Patterns (p. 56)
◇ card stock
◇ scissors
◇ snack foods such as trail mix, M&Ms, fish-shaped crackers, Hershey's Kisses, stick pretzels, etc.
◇ paper bowls
◇ plastic spoons
◇ ribbon
◇ ruler
◇ resealable sandwich-sized plastic bags
◇ heart-shaped stickers
◇ hole punch
◇ markers

SERVICE PROJECT OPTION
Children make bags to give to a senior center or an organization in the community that cares for families in need.

→ Art Center

Make a Map

Preparation

Photocopy onto white card stock one set of Places I Go Patterns for each child. Cut out.

Procedure

Children glue Places I Go Patterns to construction paper. They create maps using markers to draw lines from one place to another. Then they use markers to draw additional details.

Conversation

Today's story tells about two men who trusted God. They believed His promise to be with them wherever they went.

» Alicia, where are some places you go? Is your ballet class near your house or far away? Where are some other places you go?

» God loves us wherever we go! Our Bible says, *Be strong and courageous . . . for the Lord your God will be with you wherever you go.* These words are a promise from God. Let's say God's promise together. Children repeat verse.

Kindergarten Adaptation

Children draw roads and then make stop signs and other road signs to place on their maps.

Dramatic Play Center

Goin' on a Hike

Procedure

Children dress in hiking clothes and use equipment to pretend to go on a hike. (Optional: Children put fabric or blanket on floor to represent a river. They pretend to eat lunch next to river.)

Conversation

In our Bible story today, we will hear about Joshua and Caleb. They believed God's promise that He would be with them, even though they were going to a place they had never been before.

» Mitchell, what did you see on your hike? Where are some other places you like to go? God promises to be with us wherever we go.

» Sara, I'm glad to know that God is with us when we go on a hike. When are some other times that God is with us? (At school. At home. In the car.) God is always with us. Let's thank God for His promise to always be with us. Lead child in a simple prayer, thanking God for His promises and for always being with him or her wherever he or she goes.

Kindergarten Adaptation

Place large boxes and paper bags stuffed with newspapers around hiking area to create "mountains" and "boulders" for children to hike around.

Block Center

Promised-Land Towns

Preparation
Spread fabric on the floor to represent ground.

Procedure
Children build towns, walls and roads. They put nature items on fabric. They use Bible blocks 28-31 and toy or plastic grapes to pretend to grow large grape clusters. Children use Bible blocks 25-26 and toy people to act out traveling down the road and spying on towns they have built.

Conversation
In today's story we will hear about Joshua and Caleb. These men believed God's promise to be with them wherever they went.

>> Let's pretend Joshua and Caleb are walking down the road to see the new land God promised to give them. Michelle, what do you think they will see?

>> Our Bible says, *Be strong and courageous . . . for the Lord your God will be with you wherever you go.* Where do you like to go, Victoria? God promises to be with you at Sunday School. We can believe God's promises.

CLEANUP TIME
Signal Cleanup Time by playing a song from *SonForce Kids CD*. Involve children in cleanup by bending to their eye level, calling each child by name and giving one simple direction at a time.

For younger children, use only the activities marked ♦.

♦Song
Play "Be Strong and Courageous" from *SonForce Kids CD*. Sing song once with children. Then sing again, leading children in motions found in songbook DVD.

♦Welcome/Gadget Puppet
Puppet enters and greets children. **Today is our last day at SonForce Kids VBS. I will miss playing games with you all! In today's game you must watch carefully to see what to do next.** Children stand in a line. **I'm going to pick a leader for our line. We will all follow our leader and do whatever he or she does.** Children play a game like "Follow the Leader." Continue play until all children have had a turn to be the leader. **Thank you! You all did a great job following each other. I have to go now. Time to see what the SonForce Kids want me to do today. Bye!** Puppet exits.

At SonForce Kids VBS we've learned that God loves us and gives us many promises in His Word, the Bible. One of God's promises is that He loves us wherever we go. Let's learn a finger play that tells us God is with us wherever we go.

♦Finger Play: "God Is with Me"

Wherever I am and wherever I go,
God always goes with me.

  nod head, yes

When I'm in the car or at the park,
I know just where He'll be.

  nod head, yes

When I clean my room or play with my friend
No matter what I do,

God is with me everywhere,
And He is with you, too!

nod head, yes

Younger Child Adaptation: Omit second stanza to shorten the finger play.

Sharing
Some of you made maps today. Your maps had places you go. Troy, where are some places you go? I'm happy that God is with us wherever we go. Logan, where are some places that God goes with you?

♦Bible Verse
God promises to always be with us. Listen to what our Bible tells us: *Be strong and courageous . . . for the Lord your God will be with you wherever you go*. Let's say the verse together. Children repeat verse. **This verse means that even though we can't see Him, God is always with you! Wherever we are, God promises to be there, too!**

Song
Play "Hear the Word" from CD. Lead children in singing and doing motions found in songbook DVD.

♦Prayer
Let's thank God for loving us and for being with us, wherever we are. Lead children in prayer. **Dear God, thank You for loving us. And thank You for promising to be with us, no matter where we go! Help us to tell others about Your promises, too. In Jesus' name, amen.**

♦Transition
In our Bible story today, listen to find out about two men who believed God's promise.

◇ Bible
◇ *SonForce Kids Songbook, CD* and player
◇ Gadget Puppet

Materials Checklist

Bible Story/Application (10-15 minutes)

(Note: See "Storytelling Tips" on p. 10 for ways to present the story.)

Preparation

Before class, prefold *SFA Manual* pages to form storybooks, and then reopen pages. In class, children will find it easier to refold the page.

Use crayon or marker to draw a happy face on one paper plate and a sad face on the other. Staple each plate to a tongue depressor. At the appropriate time in the story, show happy or sad face. Children imitate face as you tell story.

Materials Checklist

◇ Bible
◇ Life of Jesus Poster from *Teaching Resources*
◇ Figures 17-21 from *Teaching Resources*
◇ *SFA Manual* Level 5 pages
◇ flannel board
◇ small cluster of grapes
◇ crayons or markers
◇ 2 paper plates
◇ 2 tongue depressors

Joshua: Spy in a Strange Land

(Hold Bible open to Numbers 13 as you expressively tell the story. Do motions and show flannel figures as indicated.)

What is your favorite fruit? Hold up a cluster of grapes. **Listen to hear about a wonderful place where God's people found huge bunches of grapes!** Set grapes aside while you read the story.

A Promised Land

God had promised to give His people a special place to live after they left Egypt. The special place was called the Promised Land. (*Show happy face.*) After many days of walking on their way to the Promised Land, God's people stopped to camp. While they were waiting, God told Moses to choose some men to go ahead of everyone else and look at the land that He promised to give them. Moses carefully chose 12 men. (*Show Figures 17 and 18.*)

"Go see the land God has promised to give us," Moses said. "Then come back and tell us about what you saw." The men were happy. (*Show happy face.*) They were going to be the first ones to get to see the wonderful place where they would be living!

A Different Story

When the men came back they had exciting news! "God has given us a wonderful place! Full of good things! See the big bunches of grapes we brought back." (*Show happy face. Show Figure 19.*)

"But," some of the men said, "the people who live there now are big and strong. The cities have large walls around them, so that we can't get in! We can never move into this land." (*Show sad face.*)

God's people were afraid when they heard the scary things the men were saying. (*Show sad face. Show Figure 20.*) They began to complain, "We can't make those people leave! They're too strong! They'll hurt us if we try to live there." (*Show sad face.*) All of God's promises didn't seem real to the people now.

A New Plan

Joshua and his friend Caleb were two of the men who had gone to see the Promised Land. (*Show Figure 21.*) Joshua and Caleb remembered that God had promised to be with them and take care of them. They told the people, "God will help us. He will give us what He promised." (*Show happy face.*) But nobody believed them. (*Show sad face. Show Figure 20.*)

Moses was sad because the people didn't trust God. (*Show Figure 17. Show sad face.*) God had promised again and again that He would give them this land. All they had to do was obey Him. And now they didn't believe God's promise! (*Show sad face.*)

Moses prayed to God, "Because You love these people, please forgive them for not believing Your promise."

God said He would forgive them! (*Show happy face. Show Figure 20.*) But because they didn't believe Him, God told His people that they would have to wait to go into the Promised Land for 40 more years. That meant the people who didn't believe God's promises and were afraid wouldn't get to live in the Promised Land. (*Show sad face.*) Their children would be the ones who would get to live there.

But what would happen to Joshua and Caleb? (*Show Figure 21.*) God said, "Since Joshua and Caleb have believed my promises, I will let them live in the Promised Land." (*Show happy face.*)

Joshua and Caleb were brave and believed God's promises, even when everyone else was afraid! And 40 years later, Joshua led God's people into the Promised Land. Joshua and Caleb knew that God keeps His promises. (*Show happy face.*)

Conclusion

Joshua and Caleb showed courage and believed God, even when things looked scary. They knew that God would keep His promise and give them a beautiful place to live. God loves us. He never, ever forgets to keep His promises! Let's pray and thank God for the good promises in the Bible. Lead children in short prayer, saying, **Thank You, God, for loving us. Thank You for all of the wonderful promises that You give us in the Bible. In Jesus' name, amen.**

New Testament Option

When Jesus lived on Earth, He helped people learn about God's love and promises. Choose one of the storytelling options found on the back of the Life of Jesus Poster to tell children how Jesus taught about God.

Application

Teachers and helpers sit at tables with children. Pass out *SFA Manual* pages and crayons or markers. Children fold pages to make mini-storybooks.

To review the Bible story, children follow along in their mini-storybooks as you read the story aloud. **What was the name of the special place God promised to give His people?** (Promised Land.) **What did the men tell the people about the Promised Land?** ("We can never move into this land.") **What did Joshua and Caleb tell the people?** ("God will help us. He will give us what He promised.") **Joshua and Caleb believed God's promise. God gives us promises in His Word, the Bible. I'm glad that we can always believe God's promises, too.**

Children unfold mini-storybook and repeat Bible verse after you. **Where does our verse say God will be with us?** (Wherever we go.) **Where are some places you go that God is with you?** Children complete "God Is with Me" activity. **God has promised to always be with us wherever we go. We can trust God to keep His promises.**

Recreation Game (10-15 minutes)

Falling Grapes

Preparation

Inflate and tie balloons. Mark a starting line using masking tape or rope. On each box, tape one different color of balloon. Place boxes at opposite end of large playing area. Randomly place half of balloons around playing area.

Procedure

In today's Bible story, Joshua and Caleb went to a country that had large bunches of grapes. Let's pretend these balloons are grapes. Grapes come in three different colors: red, green and purple. Children stand behind masking-tape line. On your signal, children run to pick up "grapes" and place them in the box with the matching grape taped to it. While children are picking up grapes, throw more into playing area so that children can catch them as they fall and take them to corresponding boxes. (Note: If any balloons break during play, be sure to pick up pieces immediately as they may present a choking hazard.)

Kindergarten Adaptation

Divide class into teams, one team for each color of balloon. (Note: Make sure that there are an equal number of balloons for each team.) Assign each team a balloon color. Place all balloons randomly about the playing area. At your signal, children race to see who can put all of their balloons in boxes first.

Materials Checklist

◇ masking tape or rope
◇ 3 large boxes
◇ 30 balloons in red, green and purple (10 of each color)

Snack (10-20 minutes)

Promised Land Picnic

Preparation

Cut fruit into small pieces. Cut cheese into cubes. Set out bottles of honey. Place fruit, cheese and crackers on separate paper plates. (Optional: Because grapes can present a choking hazard for young children, serve grapes whole only if children are four years and older. For younger children, cut grapes in half.)

Procedure

Children wash and dry hands. They place some of each food item on paper plates. They dip spoons into honey and drizzle over crackers. (Optional: If you normally eat snack indoors, take children outdoors to enjoy their Promised Land Picnic.)

Note: Check registration forms for possible food allergies and post a note alerting parents to the food items used in today's snack.

Materials Checklist

Food items—
◇ oranges and pears
◇ cheese cubes
◇ crackers
◇ squeeze bottles of honey
Optional—
◇ grapes
Utensils—
◇ scissors or kitchen shears
◇ knife
◇ paper plates
◇ napkins

Craft (15-20 minutes)

Joshua and Caleb Take a Peek

Children make Joshua and Caleb Take a Peek craft. For complete craft instructions, see *Special Agent Crafts for Kids*.

Music Fun/Good-Byes (10-15 minutes)

After children complete their crafts, guide them to the music activity area. Play CD as children gather.

Song

Play "Be Strong and Courageous" from *SonForce Kids CD*. Lead children in singing song and doing motions found in songbook DVD.

Game

Before class, cut a large circle, triangle and square shape from butcher paper and tape to floor. Children stand in a circle around shapes. Each child takes a turn to name a place where he or she likes to go and then tosses a beanbag onto shape of his or her choosing. Continue playing until each child has had several turns to name a place and toss beanbags.

Bible Verse

Hold open Bible. **Our Bible says, *Be strong and courageous . . . for the Lord your God will be with you wherever you go.*** Children repeat verse and then take turns telling a place they like to go. **This verse promises that God is always with us. That means that if we go to school, God is with us. If we are at home, God is with us. If we go to our grandma's house, God is with us. Even though we can't see Him, God is always with us.**

Prayer

Lead children in prayer. **Dear God, we thank You for Your promise to always be with us. We thank You for all of the promises You give us in Your Word. Thank You, too, for Your love. Help us show Your love to others, too. In Jesus' name, amen.**

Good-Bye

This week at SonForce Kids VBS we learned that we could always trust God and His love for us. And we learned that God has promised to be with us, wherever we go. I'm glad that God loves us and cares for us, no matter where we are. Distribute take-home materials. (Optional: Play songs from *SonForce Kids CD* and provide rhythm instruments for children to play until parents arrive.) Remind parents about your VBS Closing Program.

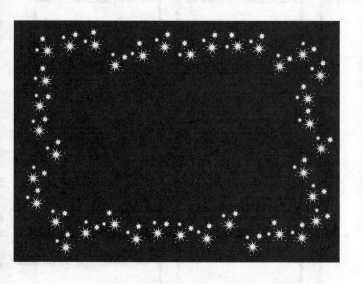

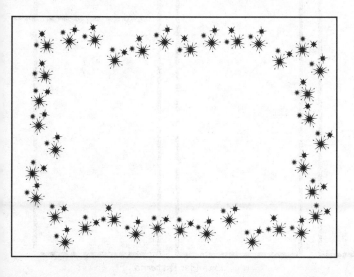

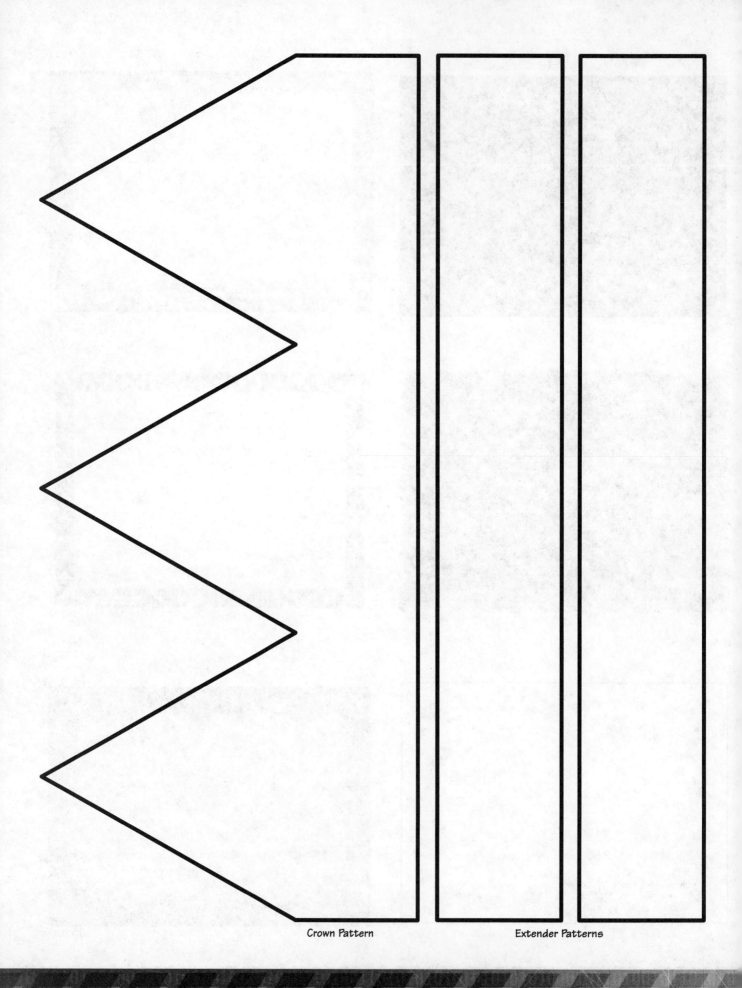

Crown Pattern

Extender Patterns

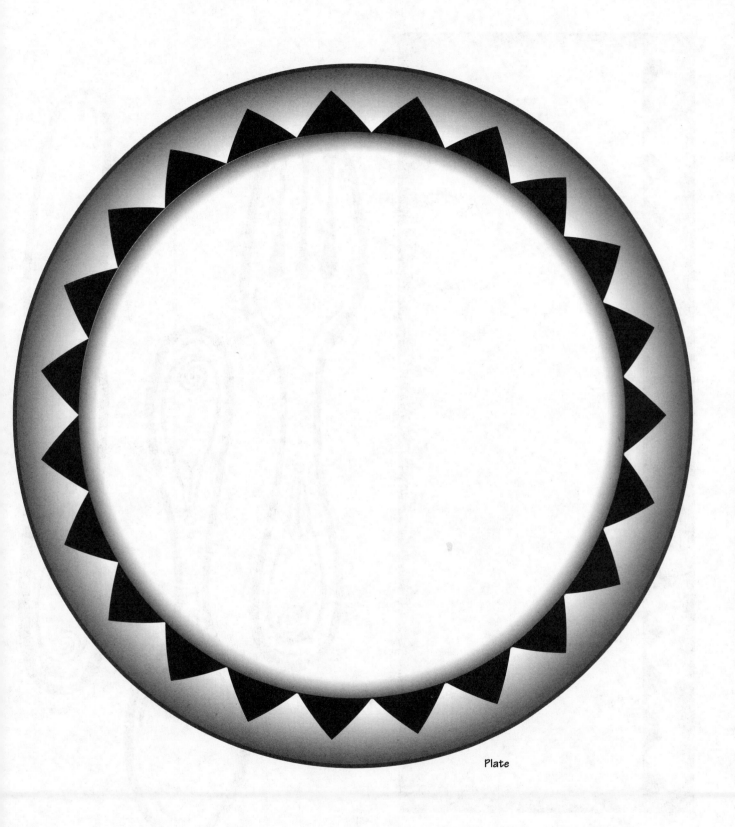

Plate

Napkin

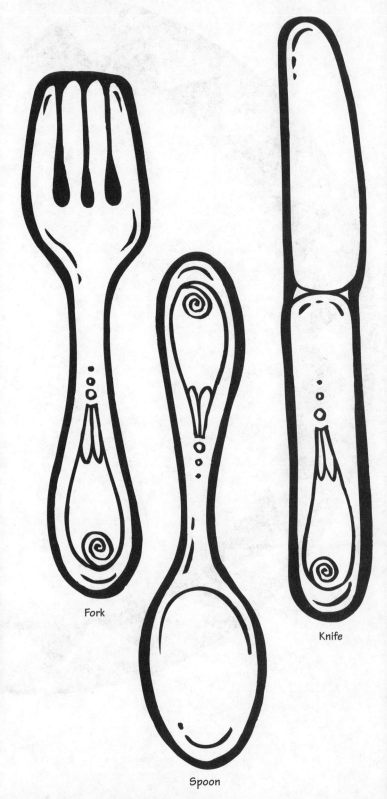

Fork

Spoon

Knife

Church

House

Playground

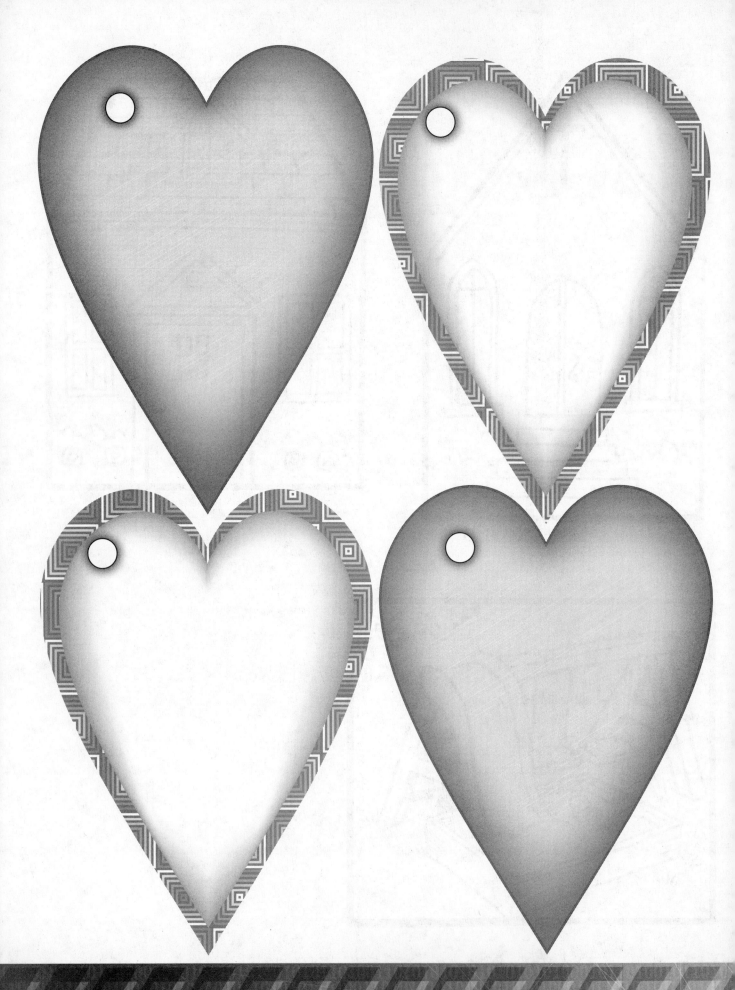